LANGUAGE DEVELOPMENT THROUGH CONTENT
AMERICA: THE EARLY YEARS

Anna Uhl Chamot

▲ Addison-Wesley Publishing Company

READING, MASSACHUSETTS • MENLO PARK, CALIFORNIA
DON MILLS, ONTARIO • WOKINGHAM, ENGLAND • AMSTERDAM
SYDNEY • SINGAPORE • TOKYO • MADRID • BOGOTA
SANTIAGO • SAN JUAN

A Publication of the World Language Division

Acknowledgments

Grateful acknowledgment is made to Lisa Küpper, Talbot Hamlin, and Elly Schottman for their contributions to this book.

Editorial: Elly Schottman, Talbot Hamlin

Production/Manufacturing: James W. Gibbons

Design: Byron Bush

Maps: EX LIBRIS

Illustrations: Susan Avishai

Photographs courtesy of: p. 8, Rafael Millán (ul)(ll); Peabody Museum, Harvard University (ur); **pp. 8 & 9,** National Archives (bkgd); Peabody Museum, Harvard University; **p. 9,** Peabody Museum, Harvard University photographs by Hillel Burger (l)(uc)(lc)(r); **p. 11,** Museum of the American Indian, Heye Foundation; **p. 15,** Department of Interior–Sport Fisheries and Wildlife; **p. 20,** Fred Bruemmer (3); **p. 22,** Department of Library Services, American Museum of Natural History (ll)(ur), Southwest Museum (lr); **p. 24,** The Library of Congress (ur), Historical Picture Service, Chicago (ul), Arizona Office of Tourism (ll); **p. 31,** National Archives; **p. 36,** National Archives photograph by Ansel Adams; **p. 39,** Texas State Archives (l), United States Department of Interior–National Park Service (ur), Montana Department of Tourism (lr); **pp. 50, 56, 58 & 59,** Plimoth Plantation photographs by Ted Avery; **p. 60,** The Pilgrim Society; **p. 68,** Bettmann Archive, Inc. (ur), C70249 the Public Archives of Canada (ll); **p. 73,** the Collection of the Library of Congress; **p. 103,** The Franklin Institute of Boston.

ISBN 0-201-12929-9

17 18 19 20 CRS 0403020100

To the Teacher

Language Development Through Content: Social Studies is specifically designed to help prepare limited English proficient students for curricular work in United States history and world geography. Through readings and language exercises, it helps them learn the language of social studies and sharpen their reading comprehension. Through exercises based on maps, charts, and graphs, it helps build important interpretive social studies skills. Through listening exercises, it builds both listening and note-taking skills. And through report development exercises, it gives students combined practice in researching, writing, and speaking, together with further reinforcement in listening and note-taking.

The content core of the two worktexts is the story of the Americas, and particularly the part that became the United States. Interwoven with this historical survey is the study of geographic regions around the world. The two worktexts are transitional and preparatory material for mainstream classes; they are not intended as substitutes for social studies textbooks. Students who complete them will have acquired invaluable language experience in an academic context. In addition, they will have made a start toward gaining the conceptual background that mainstream young people bring to their social studies courses.

The worktexts present English language as it is used in the social studies content area. The exercises preceding and following the social studies readings develop academic language skills while reinforcing understanding of the content. A basic social studies vocabulary is built (see the Glossary at the end of this book), and a variety of learning strategies and reading skills are developed and practiced. Listening comprehension in the academic context is also emphasized. In each unit students listen to a "mini-lecture" and are guided through the skill of taking notes. The texts for these "mini-lectures" are provided in the Teacher's Guide. Many of the activities in the worktexts (and many of the suggested procedures in the accompanying Teacher's Guide) involve students working in pairs or small groups, giving them maximum opportunity to use language actively. Discussion questions, as well as a variety of other activities requiring social interaction, provide creative springboards for the development of thinking skills and oral language facility.

Language Development Through Content: Social Studies can be used effectively in both the ESOL classroom and the mainstream classroom. Instructions for the student activities are clear and complete. You will wish to go over them orally with the students, however, to make sure that each student understands what he or she is to do. In addition, the Teacher's Guide presents detailed suggestions for teaching each lesson. By following these suggestions, you will be providing your students with many opportunities to use their developing English skills. You will also be helping them to build a valuable inventory of learning strategies which will carry over directly into their mainstream work. One important suggestion concerns the assignment of students to pairs or groups. Mixed (heterogeneous) grouping is recommended wherever possible so that more proficient students can provide assistance and serve as models for those who are less proficient. <u>The texts for the listening exercises are found in the Teacher's Guide only</u>. You can either read these to the students or, if you prefer, tape record them for individual use. The Guide also includes suggested answers for all exercises in the worktexts.

Language Development Through Content: Social Studies aims to teach students the language and many of the skills they will need to study social studies subjects in the mainstream curriculum. At the same time, it helps these students to learn or review some of the basic facts and concepts presented in these subjects at the upper elementary and middle school levels. It can help your students toward greater success in their mainstream classrooms.

Contents

*Teacher scripts are provided for these listening and note-taking activities in the Teacher's Guide.

Maps

*Teacher scripts are provided for these listening and note-taking activities in the Teacher's Guide.

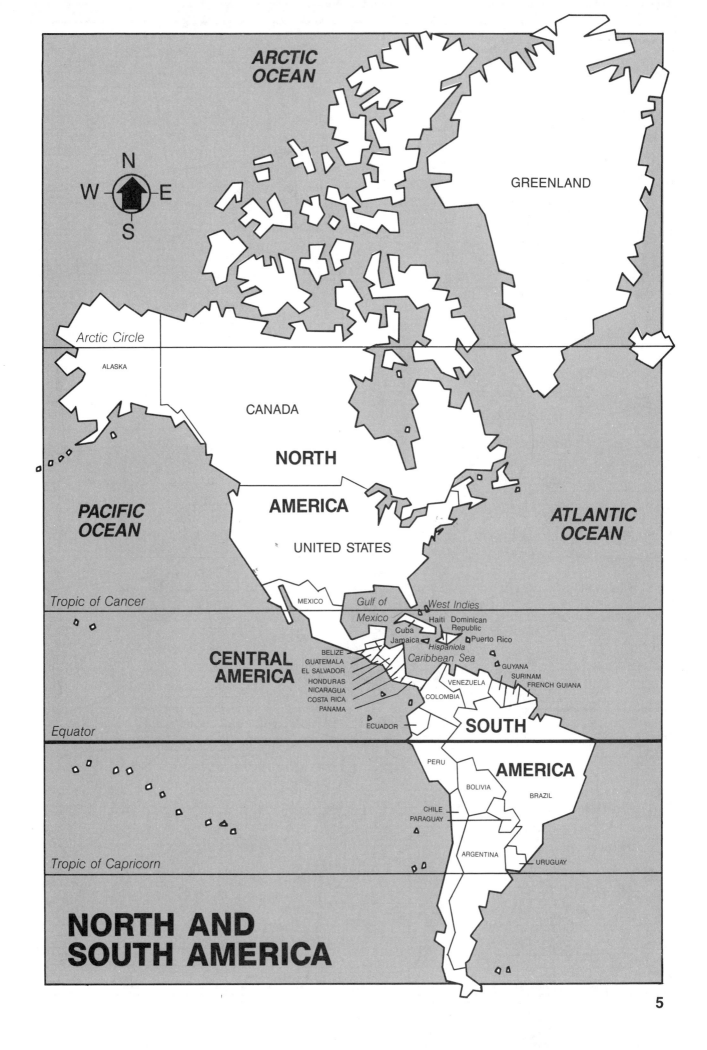

ARCTIC
OCEAN

N
W · E
S

GREENLAND

Arctic Circle

ALASKA

CANADA

NORTH

AMERICA

UNITED STATES

PACIFIC
OCEAN

ATLANTIC
OCEAN

Tropic of Cancer

MEXICO   Gulf of   West Indies
          Mexico
                    Haiti   Dominican
                            Republic
          Cuba   Puerto Rico
          Jamaica
                    Hispaniola
BELIZE   Caribbean Sea
CENTRAL   GUATEMALA   GUYANA
AMERICA   EL SALVADOR   SURINAM
               HONDURAS   FRENCH GUIANA
               NICARAGUA   VENEZUELA
               COSTA RICA   COLOMBIA
               PANAMA

Equator   ECUADOR   **SOUTH**

                PERU   **AMERICA**

                BOLIVIA
                            BRAZIL
            CHILE
        PARAGUAY

Tropic of Capricorn
            ARGENTINA   URUGUAY

NORTH AND
SOUTH AMERICA

5

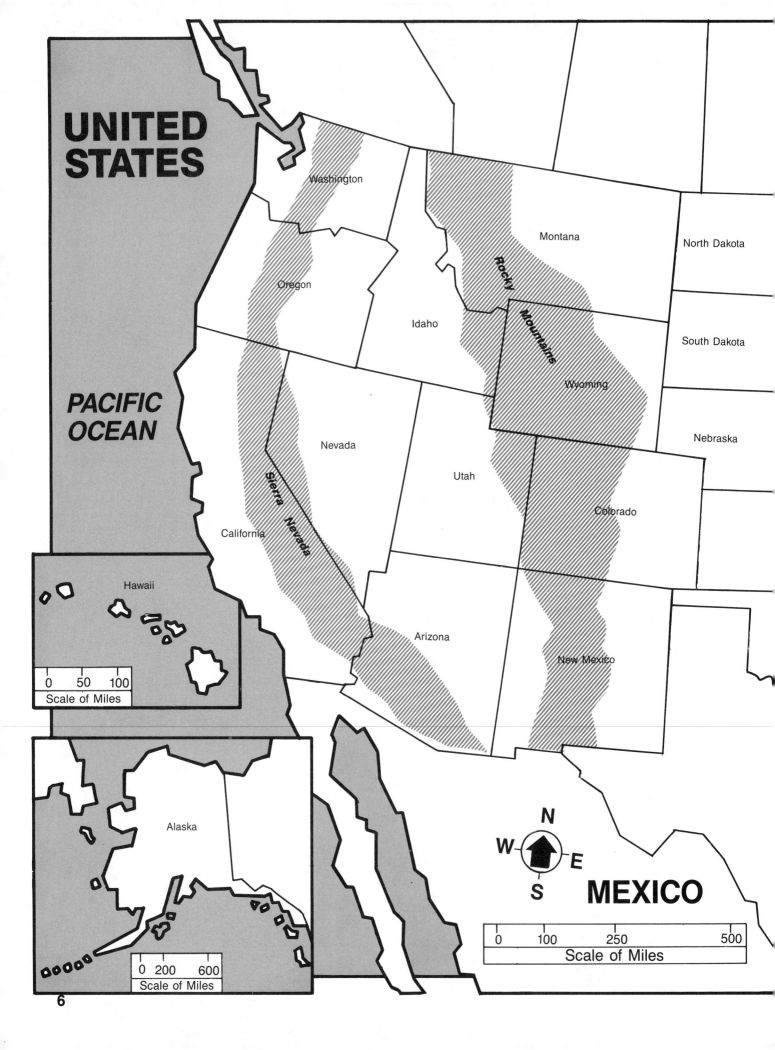

UNITED STATES

PACIFIC OCEAN

Washington

Oregon

Idaho

Montana

North Dakota

South Dakota

Wyoming

Rocky Mountains

Nevada

Sierra Nevada

Utah

Colorado

Nebraska

California

Arizona

New Mexico

Hawaii

0	50	100

Scale of Miles

Alaska

0	200	600

Scale of Miles

MEXICO

N
W E
S

0	100	250	500

Scale of Miles

6

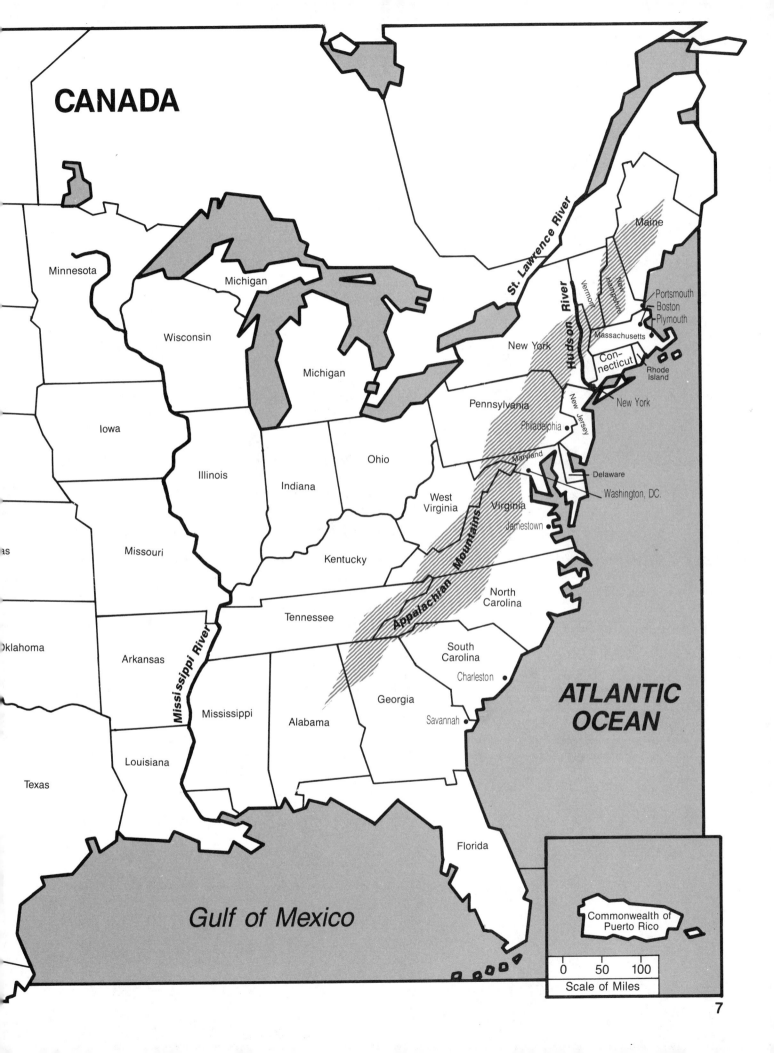

CANADA

Minnesota

Michigan

Wisconsin

Michigan

Iowa

Illinois

Indiana

Ohio

Pennsylvania

New York

St. Lawrence River

Hudson River

Vermont

New Hampshire

Maine

Portsmouth
Boston
Plymouth

Massachusetts

Con-
necticut

Rhode
Island

New York

New Jersey

Philadelphia

Maryland

Delaware

Washington, DC.

West
Virginia

Virginia

Jamestown

Missouri

Kentucky

Oklahoma

Arkansas

Tennessee

North
Carolina

South
Carolina

Charleston

Appalachian Mountains

Mississippi River

Mississippi

Alabama

Georgia

Savannah

Texas

Louisiana

Florida

ATLANTIC
OCEAN

Gulf of Mexico

Commonwealth of
Puerto Rico

| 0 | 50 | 100 |

Scale of Miles

7

The First Americans

Who were the first people to live in the Americas?

Where did they come from?

How did they live?

Unit 1

In this unit you will:

- read about the first Americans
- learn about the regions of the world
- read about life in the Polar Regions
- use bar graphs and maps
- learn about several Native American cultures
- sharpen your listening and note-taking skills

The Earliest Americans

BEFORE YOU READ: Vocabulary

PEOPLE	THINGS PEOPLE DO	OTHER WORDS	
Europeans	migrate	climate	migration
farmers	settle	continents	route
hunters		herd	

Write each vocabulary word by the correct definition. Use a dictionary or the glossary at the end of this book if you need help. Check your answers with a friend. When you are sure that your answers are correct, you can play the game below.

1. _____ A group of animals, such as cows or deer.

2. _____ People who grow food.

3. _____ To move from one place to another.

4. _____ People who live in Europe or come from Europe.

5. _____ The movement of people from one place to another.

6. _____ People who kill and eat wild animals.

7. _____ The seven large bodies of land: North America, South America, Europe, Asia, Africa, Australia and Antarctica.

8. _____ A way or path to somewhere.

9. _____ The kind of weather in a place.

10. _____ To stay and live in one place.

ACTIVITY: Vocabulary Game

Read five definitions to your friend. Your friend has to say the word that matches each definition, without looking at the book! Give one point for each correct answer. Then your friend will read the other five definitions to you, and you will say the word that matches each definition.

My friend's score	

My score	

BEFORE YOU READ: Using Section Headings

Look at the headings above each section of "The First to Come to America" (page 12). These headings are questions. They give clues about the information in the reading. Many of the words in these headings begin with capital letters. Headings often use capital letters in this special way. Copy the four headings on the lines below, but write them as regular sentences. Follow these rules:

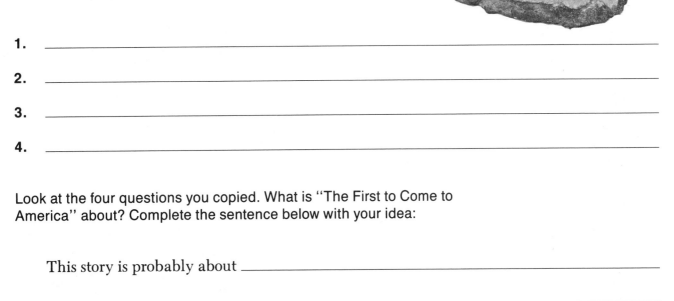

   a. Capitalize the first letter of a sentence.
      Example: It was cold.

   b. Capitalize the first letter of a nationality word.
      Example: European, Spanish, Native American

   c. Capitalize the first letter of a continent.
      Example: Asia, South America

   d. Put a question mark at the end of each question.

1. _____

2. _____

3. _____

4. _____

Look at the four questions you copied. What is "The First to Come to America" about? Complete the sentence below with your idea:

This story is probably about _____

_____

Now read page 12 to find out if you were right.

The First to Come to America

Who Were the Earliest Americans?

The earliest Americans were hunters who came from Asia. They migrated to America many thousands of years ago during the Ice Age. At that time, the earth's climate was colder than it is today. There was snow and ice all year in many parts of the Americas.

Look at the map on page 13. It shows how the land probably was during the Ice Age. There was probably a land bridge between Asia and North America. That means that a piece of land probably connected Asia and North America. The lines show the routes that the Asian hunters probably took when they came to America.

Why Did Asian Hunters Come to America?

The hunters were probably following herds of large animals. There were herds of mammoths, caribou, horses, and bison. The hunters moved to new places and settled where they could find animals to kill for food. The hunters did not grow food, and they didn't stay in one place very long.

What Happened to the Asian Hunters Who Migrated to the Americas?

These men and women settled all over North, Central, and South America. The migration probably went on for several thousand years. During that time, some of the hunters learned to farm. That means that they learned how to grow plants for food.

When Europeans first came to America, there were many tribes or groups of people already settled in different parts of the Americas. Each tribe had its own culture or way of life. Some were still hunters. Some were farmers. Some gathered wild food and also hunted; some fished. The Europeans called these tribal people "Indians." Today, we often call them Native Americans because they were the first people to settle in America.

Where Are the Native Americans Today?

There are still many Native Americans in the Americas. In the United States, some live on reservations, land used only by Native Americans. Some live in towns and cities. Some Native Americans still know how to speak their tribal languages. Most speak the same language as the people around them. In the United States, most Native Americans speak English. In Central and South American countries, most Native Americans speak Spanish. Native Americans are important in the history of the Americas. You will find out more about Native Americans in this unit.

Prehistoric horses

Mammoth

Caribou

Bison

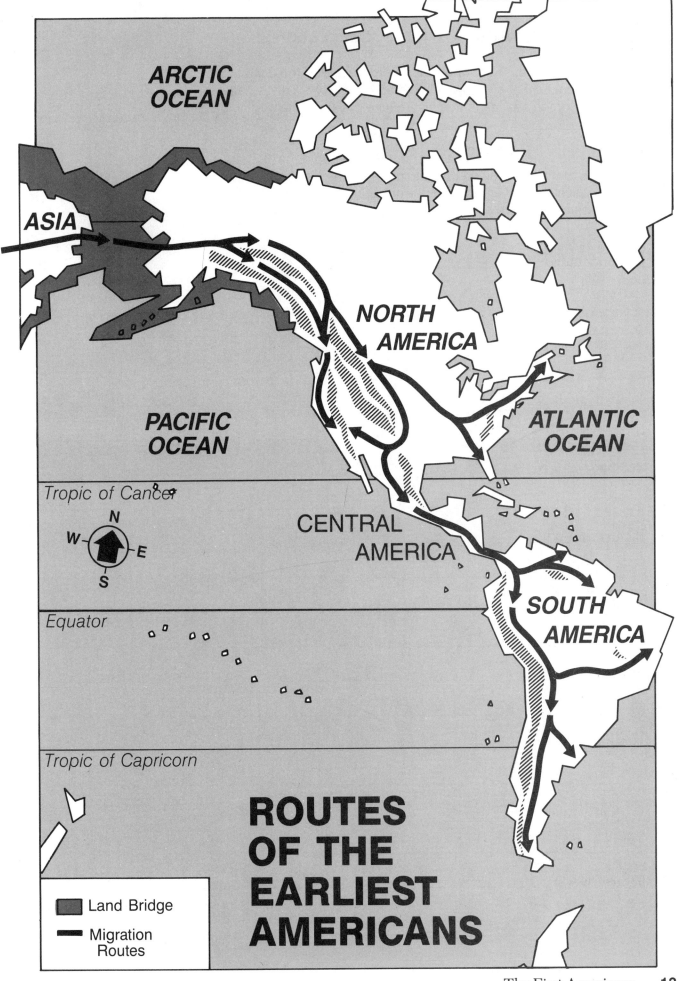

ARCTIC OCEAN

ASIA

NORTH AMERICA

PACIFIC OCEAN

ATLANTIC OCEAN

Tropic of Cancer

N
W   E
S

CENTRAL AMERICA

Equator

SOUTH AMERICA

Tropic of Capricorn

ROUTES OF THE EARLIEST AMERICANS

Land Bridge

Migration Routes

UNDERSTANDING WHAT YOU READ: Using Context

You can make good guesses about what a word means by looking at the
words and sentences that come before and after the word. This is called
using *context*. Sometimes maps and pictures help explain the meaning of
a new word, too.

Find the following words in "The Earliest Americans" on page 12. You can
also find some of these words on the map or under the pictures. Write a
definition for each word or phrase. Work with a partner or a group to make
your definitions as accurate as you can.

1. land bridge _____

_____

2. Asian _____

_____

3. mammoths, caribou, bison _____

_____

4. the Americas _____

_____

5. to farm _____

_____

6. tribe _____

_____

7. culture _____

_____

8. tribal _____

_____

9. Native American _____

_____

10. reservations _____

_____

UNDERSTANDING WHAT YOU READ: Comprehension Check

Read each statement. Write **T** for *True,* **F** for *False,* or **NG** if the information was *Not Given* in the story.

1. _____ The Asian hunters came to America when it was very warm.

2. _____ Many hunters probably walked from Asia to America.

3. _____ During the Ice Age there were herds of mammoths and caribou in Asia and North America.

4. _____ There are still large herds of caribou in North America.

5. _____ During the Ice Age, hunters killed and ate bison and horses.

6. _____ The hunters did not cook their meat.

7. _____ The Ice Age migration of people from Asia to the Americas went on for thousands of years.

8. _____ Some of the hunters went all the way to South America.

9. _____ Some hunters became farmers.

10. _____ The different tribes were always enemies.

11. _____ Europeans called the people Native Americans.

12. _____ Today, all Native Americans speak the same language.

13. _____ Today you could meet a Native American almost anywhere in the United States.

14. _____ In South America today, many Native Americans live on reservations.

15. _____ The Ice Age was 800 years ago.

WORLD REGIONS

ARCTIC OCEAN

Arctic Circle

NORTH AMERICA

PACIFIC OCEAN

ATLANTIC OCEAN

EUROPE

AFRICA

Tropic of Cancer

Equator

SOUTH AMERICA

Tropic of Capricorn

| 0 | 500 | 1000 | 2500 | 3000 |

Scale of Miles

- [Northern Forests] Northern Forests
- [Mid-latitude Forests] Mid-latitude Forests
- [Wet Tropical Forests] Wet Tropical Forests
- [Grasslands] Grasslands
- [Desert] Desert
- [Polar] Polar
- [Highlands] Highlands
- [Mediterranean] Mediterranean

Antarctic Circle

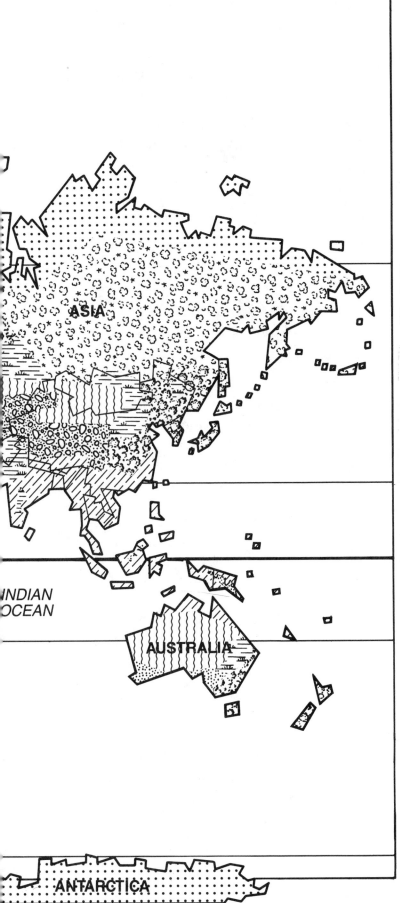

The Regions of the World

What Are Regions?

Regions are areas of the world that have similar climates, plant life, and animal life. The earth can be divided into many different regions. The map on these pages shows regions of the earth.

You will read about four of these regions: the Polar Regions, the Wet Tropical Regions, the Northern Forest Regions, and the Mid-Latitude Forest Regions.

How Are Regions Different?

Some regions, such as the Polar Regions, are always cold. Some regions, such as the Wet Tropical Regions, are always warm. Other regions, such as the Northern Forest Regions and the Mid-Latitude Forest Regions, are cold part of the year and warm other parts of the year. In the Desert Regions there is almost no rain. In the Wet Tropical Regions it rains almost every day.

People live in all the regions of the world. People in different regions usually live and work in different ways.

Regions in the United States

The United States is a very big country. It has many of the world's regions in it. When people came to what is now the United States, they settled and made homes in different regions. In each region, the homes they built were different. The clothes they made and the food they grew and caught were different, too. Towns, cities and businesses in different parts of the United States grew in different ways. These differences were partly the result of differences between the regions—differences in the land and the climate.

Look at the map and the key that shows the different regions. Find the United States on the map. Be sure to include Alaska. Find the following regions in the United States: the Polar Region, the Northern Forest Region, and the Mid-Latitude Forest Region. What is the name of the region you live in?

Now look at the rest of the world map. Where else can you find Polar Regions? Where else can you find Northern Forest Regions and Mid-Latitude Forest Regions? Where else can you find the region in which you live?

Regions of the World: The Polar Regions

Where Are the Polar Regions?

The North Pole is as far north as you can go on Earth. The South Pole is as far south as you can go on Earth. The areas around the North Pole and the South Pole are the two Polar Regions. The Polar Region around the North Pole is called the Arctic Region. The Polar Region around the South Pole is called the Antarctic Region.

Snow, Ice, and Tundra

The Polar Regions are the coldest parts of the world. Look at the maps. Almost all of the Antarctic Region is frozen all year round. The land and ocean are always covered with deep ice and snow. The ice covering the Antarctic Ocean is more than one mile deep!

Many parts of the Arctic Region are also always covered with ice and snow. However, some land in the Arctic is not frozen all year round. The top layer of some land unfreezes in the summer months. This land is called the *tundra*. In the summer, small flowers and plants grow on the tundra. Even in the tundra, however, the ground under the top layer stays frozen all year.

The Lands of the Midnight Sun

The Polar Regions are sometimes called "The Lands of the Midnight Sun." In late June, there is daylight for 24 hours, all day and all night, at the North Pole. At the same time, there is darkness all day and all night at the South Pole. In late December, the North Pole has 24 hours of darkness. At the South Pole it is light all day and all night.

Do People Live in the Polar Regions?

No people make their homes in the Antarctic Region. People do live in the Arctic Region, however. The Eskimos are a Native American people who have lived in the Arctic Regions for thousands of years. The Eskimos hunt the seals, whales, and walruses that live in the Arctic Ocean. Today, many Eskimos live in small towns near the Arctic Ocean.

Other people live in these towns as well. The people have many different jobs. Airplanes are used a lot in the Arctic Region, so some people are airplane mechanics and pilots. Oil wells are being drilled in the tundra. Many people work at the oil wells.

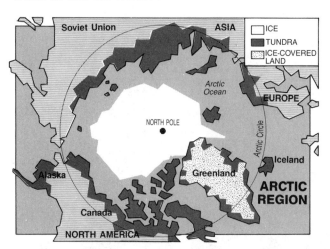

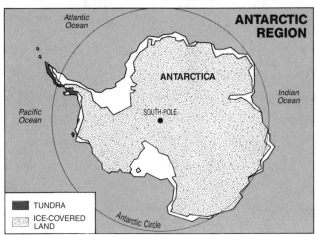

MAP SKILLS

Study the maps of the Arctic and the Antarctic Regions. Answer the questions below.

1. What part of the United States is partly inside the Arctic Region?

   _____

2. Is there more tundra in the Arctic or Antarctic polar region?

   _____

UNDERSTANDING BAR GRAPHS: Temperatures in the Polar Regions

Study the temperature graphs and think about the information in the reading.
Use the graphs and the information to answer the questions. (The letters
at the bottom of each graph stand for the months of the year, starting with
January.)

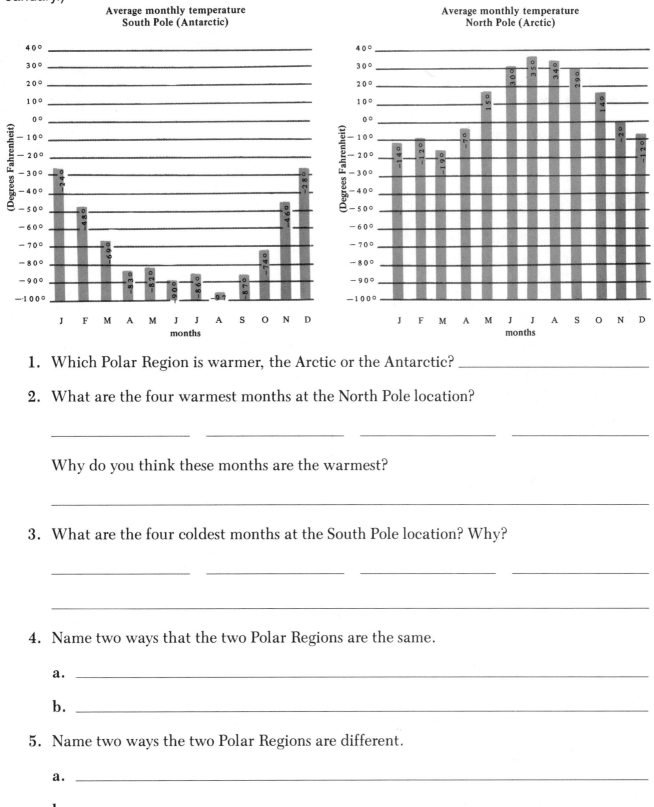

Average monthly temperature
South Pole (Antarctic)

Average monthly temperature
North Pole (Arctic)

1. Which Polar Region is warmer, the Arctic or the Antarctic? _____

2. What are the four warmest months at the North Pole location?

   _____   _____   _____   _____

   Why do you think these months are the warmest?

   _____

3. What are the four coldest months at the South Pole location? Why?

   _____   _____   _____   _____

   _____

4. Name two ways that the two Polar Regions are the same.

   a. _____

   b. _____

5. Name two ways the two Polar Regions are different.

   a. _____

   b. _____

The Eskimos

LISTENING AND TAKING NOTES

Look at the *T-List* below. A *T-List* helps you take notes on information you hear or read.

| On a T-List, the main ideas are on the left; | the details or examples are on the right. |

This *T-List* is about the Eskimos. The main ideas on the left are already complete. You are going to listen to some information about the Eskimos.

- Listen carefully and complete the details on the right.
- When you have finished, read all the information silently.

MAIN IDEAS	DETAILS AND EXAMPLES
A. Early Eskimos crossed land bridge from Asia to America thousands of years ago. 	1. Early Eskimos were last group of Asian _____ to cross land bridge. 2. Eskimos did not _____ south. 3. Today Eskimos live in North American polar regions of _____ and _____ .
B. Eskimos learned to find food in cold Arctic region.	1. Eskimos hunted sea animals such as _____ and _____ . 2. Hunted large _____ animals such as caribou and polar bears.
C. Eskimos learned to keep warm in a very cold climate. 	1. Eskimos learned to make warm _____ and build special _____ . 2. Eskimos used _____ of animals they killed to make warm clothes. 3. Some Eskimos made tents from animal _____ . 4. Some Eskimos made houses from _____ bones and grass and dirt. 5. Some Canadian Eskimos built houses of _____ . Eskimo houses are called igloos.

Some Native American Cultures

MAP SKILLS

When we talk about the culture of a group of people, we mean the whole way of life of those people. On the next two pages, you will read about the culture of some Native American Indian groups. First look at this map. It shows where some groups of Native American Indians settled. The names of the places on the map are the names we use today. Use the map to complete the paragraphs.

About 2,000 years ago, the Mayas settled in an area that today is part of several countries. The Mayan culture was centered in the south-

eastern part of _____ and in the

country of _____ .

Many years later, the Aztec people settled in the region that is now the country of

_____ .

The Incas were another group of Native American Indians. The Incan culture and the Aztec culture were powerful at the same time. The Incas lived in South America, mostly in the area that today is the country of

_____ . Many Incas still live there.

When people from Europe first came to North America, many different groups of Native American Indians lived in the area that is today Canada and the United States. Three of these groups are shown on the map.

One group of Native American Indian tribes who lived in the eastern forests of North Amer-

ica were the_____ .

An important Native American Indian tribe that still lives in the southwestern part of the

United States is the _____ tribe.

The Native American people who settled in the polar region of Alaska and Canada are

called the _____ .

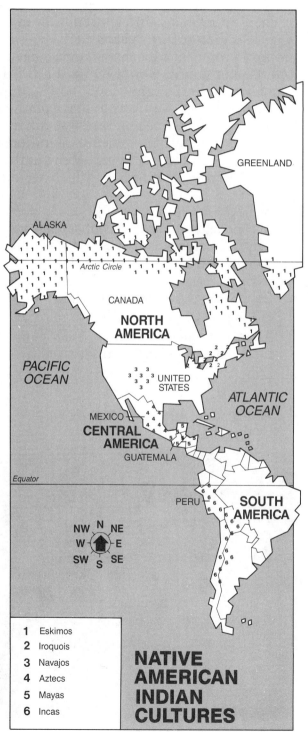

1 Eskimos
2 Iroquois
3 Navajos
4 Aztecs
5 Mayas
6 Incas

NATIVE AMERICAN INDIAN CULTURES

UNDERSTANDING WHAT YOU READ: Main Ideas

You can understand what you read better if you know how to find main ideas. As you read, ask yourself, "What is the most important point in this paragraph or part of a story? What is the one thing I should be sure to remember?"

Read the paragraphs about Indian cultures. The exercises below the paragraphs will help you find the main ideas.

Aztec emperor Montezuma meets Spanish leader Cortés

Paragraph 1

There were many different cultures in the Americas before Europeans arrived. Each group of people, or tribe, had its own language and its own special way of living. Each tribe knew how to find or grow food, how to build shelters or houses, and how to make plans for the future. Each tribe's culture was different from most other tribes'. Each was different from European ways of living. Many of these Native American cultures are still alive today.

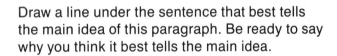

A Mayan building

Paragraph 2

The three most important Indian cultures in Central and South America were the Mayas, the Aztecs, and the Incas. The Mayas lived in parts of what is now Mexico and Central America. The Mayas were good farmers, and they knew how to study the stars. The Aztecs were powerful fighters in Central Mexico. They built a beautiful city in the place where Mexico City is today. The Incas lived in the Andes mountains in South America. They built roads and bridges in the mountains. These three important Indian cultures made statues, pottery, and jewelry that we can see today in museums. We can also visit and study the ruins of the cities they built.

Draw a line under the sentence that best tells the main idea of this paragraph. Be ready to say why you think it best tells the main idea.

a. Each Native American tribe had a different language.

b. There were many different American cultures before the Europeans arrived.

c. Many of these Native American cultures still exist today.

d. Many of the groups knew how to grow food.

Incan statues

Draw a line under the sentence that best tells the main idea of this paragraph. Be ready to tell why you chose it.

a. The Mayas, the Aztecs, and the Incas all made statues, pottery, and gold jewelry that we can see in museums today.

b. The Incas were good builders.

c. There were three important Indian cultures in Central and South America: the Mayas, the Aztecs, and the Incas.

d. The Aztecs lived in Central Mexico.

e. The Mayas studied the stars.

The End of the Aztec Empire

A Rich and Powerful Culture

The Aztecs were powerful fighters. Their large armies conquered the other Indian tribes. They controlled all of what is now Mexico. They built a beautiful city called Tenochtitlán. The city was huge and rich. It had many palaces and lovely gardens.

The Legend

The Aztecs believed in a legend, or very old story. It was about a bearded god named Quetzalcoatl. He had gone away from his people. He promised to return in 400 years. The 400 years had passed. It was the year 1519.

The Conquerors

Montezuma was the Aztec emperor in 1519. One day he received some exciting news. A group of men had landed on the coast. They had strange clothes, and their leader wore a beard! Montezuma believed that Quetzalcoatl had returned. He decided to welcome the strangers, not to fight them. He had made a big mistake. The strangers were Spanish soldiers. Their leader was Hernando Cortés. Cortés knew about the rich and powerful Aztecs. He wanted to conquer them for Spain. He expected a terrible battle.

In the City

When Cortés and his small army reached Tenochtitlán, they were very surprised. The Aztecs welcomed them in peace. Montezuma treated Cortés like a god. Cortés couldn't understand it. He became nervous. There were so many Aztecs, and so few Spanish soldiers. Cortés and his men were living in a palace. Cortés asked Montezuma to "be his guest" and live in the same palace. Montezuma agreed; he did not realize he was really a prisoner of the Spanish conqueror.

Soon, the peace was broken. The Spanish soldiers killed some Aztec chiefs. The Aztec people became angry. They attacked the soldiers. Cortés ordered Montezuma to tell the Aztecs to stop fighting. Montezuma tried, but his people wouldn't listen. They threw stones at him and killed him. The Spanish were forced to leave the city.

The Final Battle

Almost a year passed. Cortés planned his return; he built up his army. He marched back to Tenochtitlán. A terrible battle took place. The beautiful city was destroyed. Many Aztecs were killed. It was the end of the Aztec Empire. Spain had conquered Mexico.

UNDERSTANDING WHAT YOU READ: What Do You Think?

Read and discuss the questions below with one or two friends. All of the questions are *why* questions. A *why* question asks about the reasons for something. Answer the questions in complete sentences.

1. Why was Montezuma friendly to Cortés?

_____

2. Why did Cortés want to conquer the Aztecs?

_____

3. Why did Cortés become nervous?

_____

4. Why do you think the Aztecs killed Montezuma?

_____

The Iroquois and the Navajos

LISTENING AND TAKING NOTES

Here is another *T-List.* Remember, the main ideas are on the left. The details or examples are on the right.

- Listen to some information about two North American Indian cultures.

- Complete the details on the right. Notice that the details are not all written in complete sentences. When you take notes, you can write key words only. This is a kind of "shorthand." It helps you concentrate on the most important words.

MAIN IDEAS	DETAILS AND EXAMPLES
A. The Iroquois learned to live in peace. 	1. Iroquois Indians lived in _____ . 2. Food from _____ , _____ , and _____ . 3. For many years, Iroquois tribes had _____ . 4. Different _____ members of "The League of Great Peace." 5. Council arguments settled by _____ chiefs.
B. The Navajos learned to use domestic animals in a desert region. 	1. Navajos live in _____ , states of _____ and _____ . 2. Hunting and fishing difficult in _____ . 3. Spanish explorers brought _____ , _____ , and _____ . 4. The Navajos became an important _____ in the _____ .
C. Conclusion: Early Americans learned different ways to make their lives better.	1. The _____ learned to live in peace. 2. The _____ learned how to use domestic animals.

Foods Native to the Americas

Many of the foods you eat were discovered and grown by early American Indians.

POTATOES

CORN

PINEAPPLE

SWEET POTATO

AVOCADO

PUMPKIN

PEANUTS

LIMA BEANS

PEPPER

SQUASH

TOMATO

MANIOC

1. Which of these foods have you eaten? _____

_____

2. Which of these foods haven't you eaten? _____

_____

3. Think of other food you eat. Which ones would be unknown to early American Indians?

_____

ACTIVITY: Classifying and Alphabetizing

1. Work in small groups. On a separate piece of paper, make two headings:
   Food We Eat Raw and *Food We Eat Cooked.* Put all the foods above under
   one or the other heading. (Some food can go under both headings.)
   Putting words into groups is called *classifying*.

2. When you have finished classifying the words, write the lists once more
   in alphabetical order below.

Food We Eat Raw   **Food We Eat Cooked**

_____   _____   _____

_____   _____   _____

_____   _____   _____

_____   _____   _____

_____   _____   _____

_____   _____   _____

A. Circle the letter of the correct answer.

1. The first Americans were:
   a. Spanish soldiers   **b.** Aztecs   **c.** Asian hunters

2. When people *migrate*, it means that they:
   a. stay in the same place   **b.** move to a different place
   c. spend the winter in a warm place

3. The first Americans settled:
   a. all over the Americas   **b.** only in Alaska and Canada   **c.** only in Central America

4. There were many Indian *tribes* in America. This means that:
   a. All American Indians (Native Americans) spoke the same language.
   b. Many Native Americans were hunters.
   c. There were different groups of Native Americans.

5. An important Native American culture in the area that is now Peru was the:
   a. Incan   **b.** Eskimo   **c.** Mayan

6. Two important Native American cultures in Mexico and Central America were the:
   a. Incan and Aztec   **b.** Aztec and Mayan   **c.** Mayan and Incan

7. Which sentence is *not* true?
   a. The Aztecs built a beautiful city called Tenochtitlán.
   b. Cortés was a famous Aztec leader.
   c. The Aztecs lived in the area that is now Mexico.

8. An important group of Indian tribes in the area that is now New York State was the:
   a. Incas   **b.** Navajo   **c.** Iroquois

9. The Eskimos learned how to:
   a. live in a very cold climate   **b.** farm and grow corn   **c.** fight with other tribes

10. The Navajos lived in an area that is very:
    a. rainy   **b.** cold   **c.** dry

11. Montezuma was killed by:
    a. Spanish soldiers   **b.** Cortés   **c.** Aztecs

12. Areas of the world that have similar climates, animals, and plants are called:
    a. regions   **b.** reservations   **c.** continents

B. Check the words that tell about the Polar Regions.

_____ midnight sun	_____ tundra	_____ Antarctica
_____ cows, horses, sheep	_____ Eskimos	_____ The League of Great Peace
_____ fur clothing	_____ big cities	_____ igloos
_____ warm	_____ snow	_____ 24 hour darkness
_____ cold	_____ forests	_____ desert

C. Find the following places on the map and write their names on the lines.

Antarctic Region   Central America   South America

Arctic Region   North America   Asia

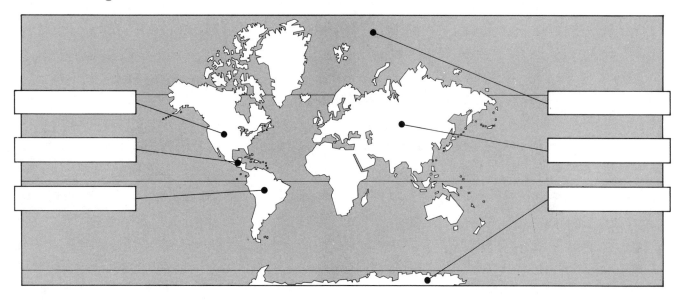

D. What Do You Think?

Discuss these questions with a friend, a small group, or the class. These are "thought questions." They do not have simple right or wrong answers.

1. Why do you think Asian hunters crossed the land bridge to North America during the Ice Age?

2. Why do you think Cortés destroyed the city of Tenochtitlán after he conquered the Aztecs?

3. Why do you think the Iroquois tribes stopped fighting and formed the League of Great Peace?

4. Why do you think the Eskimos decided to settle in the cold Arctic region?

E. Role-Play

Imagine you are in Tenochtitlán in 1519, when Cortés and the Spanish soldiers arrived. Write conversations you think might have taken place between the following people. Work with a small group of friends. Different groups can write different conversations. After you have written and practiced your conversations, people in your group can perform these short plays for the class.

1. A conversation between Montezuma and the Aztec people when they first hear about the Spanish soldiers.

2. A conversation between Montezuma and Cortés when they first meet in Tenochtitlán.

3. A conversation between Cortés and Montezuma when Montezuma is made a prisoner.

4. A conversation between Montezuma and the Aztec people. He asks them to stop attacking the Spanish soldiers.

Exploration of the New World

In this unit you will:
- read about the early explorers
- learn about the parts of America they explored
- learn why the explorations were important
- read about the Wet Tropical Regions and the Northern Forest Regions
- make bar graphs and use maps
- sharpen your listening and note-taking skills
- improve your reporting skills

Where did the early explorers come from?

Why did they come?

What did they find?

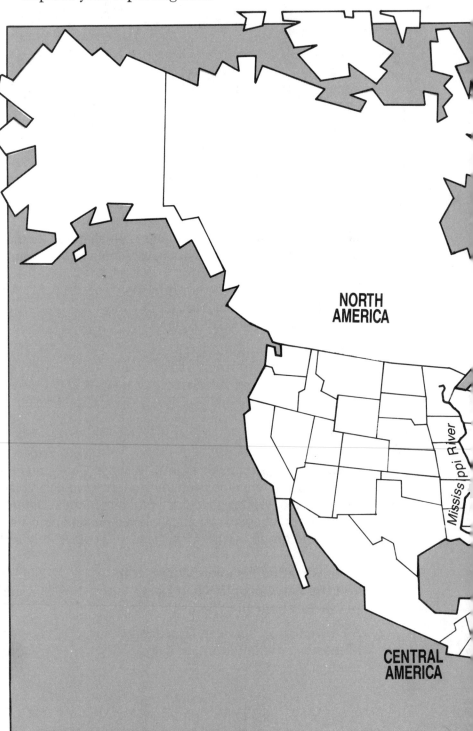

NORTH AMERICA

Mississippi River

CENTRAL AMERICA

The first Americans migrated from Asia during the Ice Age. Many thousands of years later, people came to America from Europe. They explored areas that are now parts of the United States, Mexico and Canada. They also explored many of the islands in the Caribbean Sea.

The explorers you will learn about came from Scandinavia, Spain, England, France, and the Netherlands. (Scandinavia includes Norway, Sweden, and Denmark.)

Unit Map

- Find these parts of Europe on the map.

- Color each country or area a different color.

- Color the small box in the map key to match.

- Check your work with a friend.

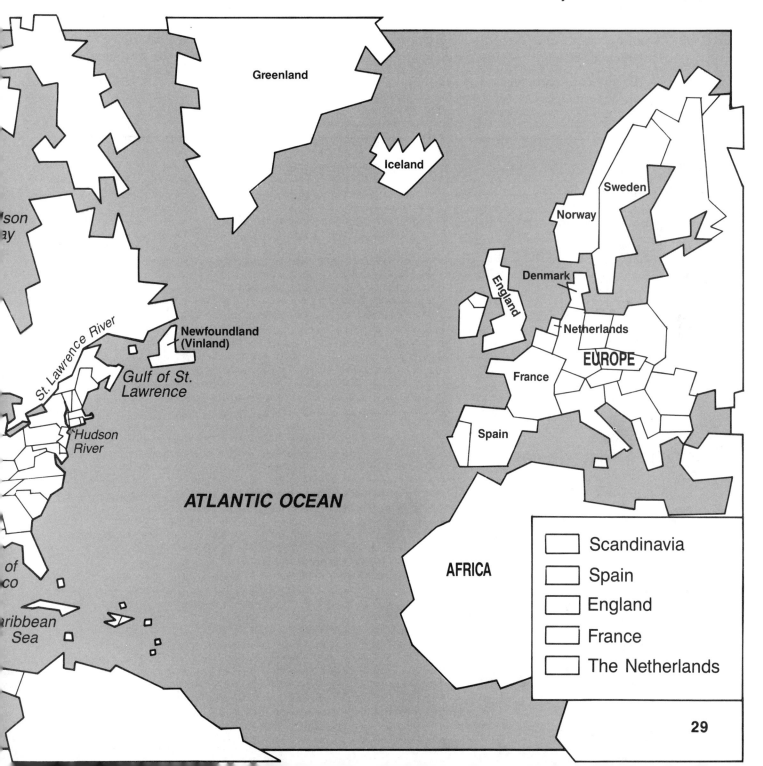

Greenland

Iceland

Sweden

Norway

Denmark

England

Netherlands

EUROPE

France

Spain

'son ay

St. Lawrence River

Newfoundland (Vinland)

Gulf of St. Lawrence

Hudson River

ATLANTIC OCEAN

of co

AFRICA

ribbean Sea

	Scandinavia
	Spain
	England
	France
	The Netherlands

The Vikings: First in North America

BEFORE YOU READ: Vocabulary

A. You will need to understand the meanings of these words for the next
reading. Study the words and their definitions. If you do not understand
a definition, ask a classmate or your teacher.

1. The **coast**: the land next to the ocean or sea.

2. **Colonists**: people from Europe who settled in America.

3. A **colony**: a place in America where Europeans settled.

4. To **discover**: to come upon, or find before anyone else.

5. To **explore**: to travel to a new place and learn more about it.

6. An **explorer**: someone who travels to unknown places and discovers new things.

7. An **ocean**: a very large body of salt water. **Oceans** cover 70% of the earth's surface.

8. To **sail**: to travel in a boat or ship that is pushed by the wind.

9. A **sailor**: a person who works on a ship.

B. You can learn new words more easily if you put them in groups, or **classify**
them, according to their meanings.

Decide which group each word should go into. Write your three groups of
words on a separate piece of paper. Then write each group of words
alphabetically below. The first word in each group has been done for you.

People	Things People Do	Places and Things
colonists	discover	coast

ACTIVITY: Viking Runes

The Vikings lived in Scandinavia many hundreds of years ago. They were
brave sailors and they traveled to many places. The Vikings had an alphabet
with letters called runes. The Vikings carved names and words in stones.
Stones with words written in runes have been found in Scandinavia and in
other countries the Vikings visited long ago. The Viking alphabet is shown
below. Use the runes to write a secret message to a friend.

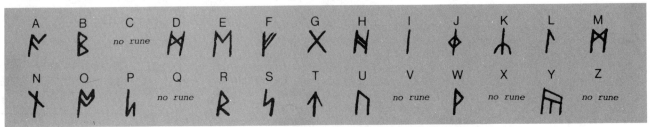

Who Were the Vikings?

The first Europeans who came to America were the Vikings. The Vikings came from Scandinavia.

They were excellent sailors. They explored the north Atlantic Ocean. They established colonies in several northern lands. They left people there to settle the land. First, the Vikings established a colony in Iceland. Then they established a colony in Greenland.

The First American Colony

In the year 1001, a Viking explorer named Leif Ericson sailed west from Greenland. He landed on the coast of North America in what is part of Canada today. He established a colony there and called it Vinland. Life was very difficult in Vinland. After a number of years, the Viking colonists went back to Greenland and Scandinavia.

The Vinland Colony Is Forgotten

Four hundred years later, no one in Europe remembered the colony of Vinland. Columbus and other European explorers in the 1400s did not know that the continents of North and South America were located west of the Atlantic Ocean.

UNDERSTANDING WHAT YOU READ: Using Maps

Go back to the map on page 29. Draw lines to show how the Vikings traveled from their home to America.

1. Draw a line from Scandinavia across the Atlantic Ocean to Iceland.

2. Draw a line from Iceland to the southern part of Greenland.

3. Finally, draw a line from Greenland to Vinland, in Canada.

4. Now color Iceland, Greenland, and Vinland the same color as Scandinavia.

Christopher Columbus

BEFORE YOU BEGIN: Vocabulary

Write the correct word in each sentence. Use a dictionary or the glossary at the end of this book, if you need help. Check your answers with a friend.

claimed	island	navigation	port	trade

1. They sailed to an _____ in the middle of the lake.

2. People who study _____ can read maps and direct a ship across the ocean.

3. When there is _____ between two countries, it means that the countries buy things from each other.

4. The ship sailed into the _____ , and the sailors spent the day in town.

5. When Columbus _____ San Salvador for Spain, he said that San Salvador belonged to Spain.

BEFORE YOU BEGIN: Using Maps

You are going to listen to some information about Christopher Columbus. First, study the map below. It shows the route Columbus followed to the New World and back to Spain. Try to keep the route in mind as you complete the *T-List* on the next page.

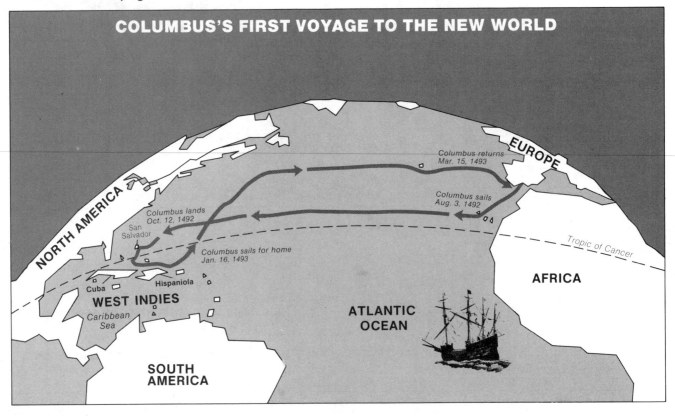

LISTENING AND TAKING NOTES

- Listen carefully to the information about Columbus.

- Complete the details on the right of the *T-List*. When you have finished, read all the information silently.

MAIN IDEAS	DETAILS AND EXAMPLES
A. Columbus's early life good preparation for his voyages.	1. Columbus born in _____ in _____. (place) (year) 2. Columbus became a _____. 3. Wanted to find new route to _____.
B. Columbus wanted to find better route to Indies by sailing west around the world.	1. In 1400s, goods from Indies carried on _____ to Middle East ports on the Mediterranean. 2. Europeans looking for _____ route to Indies. 3. Columbus wanted to sail across the _____ to the Indies.
C. Columbus reached America, thought it was the Indies. Claimed the land for Spain. 	1. Queen Isabella of _____ gave Columbus money for voyage. 2. Columbus reached America in _____. (year) 3. Thought he was in the _____ ; called the people _____ . 4. Columbus made _____ voyages to the New World. 5. Claimed land for _____ in Central and South America. 6. Established _____ on Hispaniola.
D. Columbus's voyages important for two main reasons: European knowledge of America; Spanish claims and spread of Spanish culture.	1. Europeans became interested in the New World for _____ and _____ . 2. Columbus claimed all land he found for _____ and established the 1st Spanish colony. Colonies meant Spanish _____ , _____ and _____ became important in New World.

Regions of the World: The Wet Tropical Regions

What Is a Wet Tropical Region?

When Columbus explored Cuba and Hispaniola, he found a region of green forests full of plants and animals. It rained almost every day, and it was always warm. Cuba and Hispaniola are Wet Tropical Regions. Because the weather is warm and wet, the forest is always green, and plants grow quickly.

Where Are the Wet Tropical Regions?

Wet Tropical Regions are found close to the equator, the imaginary line around the middle of the earth. Most Wet Tropical Regions are between the Tropic of Cancer and the Tropic of Capricorn. These are two other imaginary lines around the earth. They are north and south of the equator.

Life in this Region

Most people in the Wet Tropical Regions live in cities and in farm villages. In most Wet Tropical Regions there are plantations. Plantations are large farms where only one crop is grown. In the Wet Tropical Regions of Africa, there are banana, tea, cacao (chocolate), sugar cane, coffee, and manioc plantations. In the Wet Tropical Regions of Asia, there are large rubber and coconut plantations and rice paddies or fields. In the Wet Tropical Region of Puerto Rico, there are sugar cane, coffee, and banana plantations.

MAP SKILLS

Use the map to help you write short answers to the following questions.

1. Which continents have Wet Tropical Regions? _____

   _____

2. Which state in the North American part of the United States has a Wet Tropical Region? (Hint: Look at this map and the map on pages 6–7.)

   _____

3. Does Spain have Wet Tropical Regions? (Hint: Look at the map on page 29.)

   _____

4. What country do you come from?

   _____

   Is it near the equator? _____

   Is there a Wet Tropical Region there?

   _____

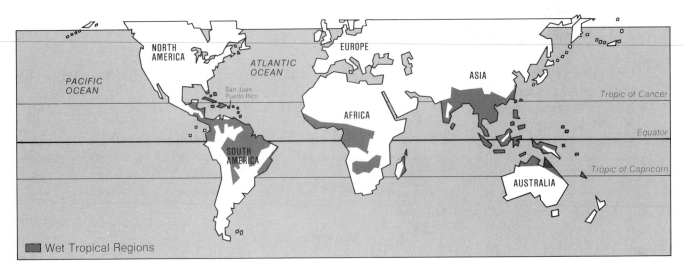

Wet Tropical Regions

MAKING BAR GRAPHS: The Climate of San Juan, Puerto Rico

You are going to make two bar graphs about the climate of San Juan, Puerto Rico. Puerto Rico is in a Wet Tropical Region. Your first bar graph will show the average temperature month by month. The second bar graph will show the average rainfall each month. The chart below gives you the facts you need for your graphs. (Remember that the letters under each graph stand for the names of the months, starting with January.) The first two months are done for you.

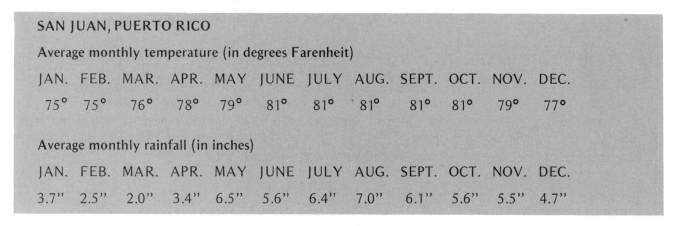

SAN JUAN, PUERTO RICO

Average monthly temperature (in degrees Farenheit)

JAN.	FEB.	MAR.	APR.	MAY	JUNE	JULY	AUG.	SEPT.	OCT.	NOV.	DEC.
75°	75°	76°	78°	79°	81°	81°	81°	81°	81°	79°	77°

Average monthly rainfall (in inches)

JAN.	FEB.	MAR.	APR.	MAY	JUNE	JULY	AUG.	SEPT.	OCT.	NOV.	DEC.
3.7"	2.5"	2.0"	3.4"	6.5"	5.6"	6.4"	7.0"	6.1"	5.6"	5.5"	4.7"

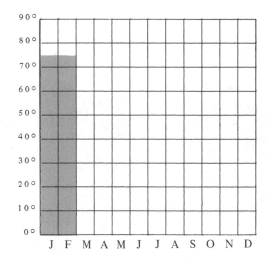

AVERAGE MONTHLY TEMPERATURE

AVERAGE MONTHLY RAINFALL

Now answer the questions below.

1. Circle the statement that is true.
   a. In San Juan, the winter is much colder than the summer.
   b. In San Juan, the summer is much colder than the winter.
   c. In San Juan, the temperature is about the same all year round.

2. In which month does San Juan get the most rainfall? _____

3. In which month does San Juan get the least rainfall? _____

4. Do you think it snows very often in San Juan? _____ Why or why not?

_____

Spanish Explorers in North America

BEFORE YOU READ: Vocabulary

Match the definitions to the words. Write the letter of the correct definition on each line.
Use a dictionary or the glossary if you need help. Check your answers with a friend.

1. capture _____

2. companion _____

3. desert _____

4. expedition _____

5. priest _____

6. in the distance _____

7. slave _____

8. territory _____

a. a very dry, hot region with lots of sand

b. a church leader

c. to take hold of a person and not let him or her go free

d. a person who is owned by someone, a person who is not free

e. a person who goes with someone

f. a journey or exploration

g. land or area

h. far away

Estevan

Spanish Rule in Mexico

After Cortés conquered the Aztecs, the Spanish ruled Mexico. They built a new city on the ruins of Tenochtitlán, the Aztec capital. The Spanish sent explorers both north and south to claim new lands and find more gold for Spain.

One of the earliest explorers for the Spanish in America was a black African slave named Estevan. On one expedition to the area that is now Texas, Estevan and his companions were captured by Indians. While Estevan was a prisoner of the Indians, he learned their language. He heard legends about seven wonderful cities of gold.

Estevan and his companions escaped from the Indians and returned to Mexico City. Estevan retold the legends about the seven cities of gold.

In Search of the Cities of Gold

In 1539, an expedition went north to search for the seven gold cities. The leader of the expedition was Fray Marcos, a Spanish priest. But

Estevan was the most important member of the group. He could speak the Indian language. He understood the Indian life. Most of all, he was very brave and very determined to find the legendary cities of gold.

The Expedition Ends

The expedition reached the desert area that today is New Mexico and Arizona. Even Estevan had not been in these lands. One day Fray Marcos sent Estevan and a few men ahead of the main group. Estevan and his men were never seen again.

When Estevan didn't return to the main expedition, Fray Marcos went out to look for him. The desert sun was high in the sky. Marcos saw an Indian village in the distance. The sun was shining very brightly. The roofs of the village looked like gold. Fray Marcos thought the search was over. He thought he had found a city of gold. He returned to Mexico City. He said that the expedition had found one of the cities of gold.

The Search Continues

The Spanish in Mexico City were very, very happy to hear Fray Marcos's news. They sent more expeditions north. They wanted to establish colonies there. They continued to search for the legendary cities of gold. But they never found them. They did claim the territories of New Mexico and Arizona for Spain. Spain now ruled much of the New World.

UNDERSTANDING WHAT YOU READ: Using Maps

Estevan and Fray Marcos explored and claimed the area of two states for Spain. Find the names of the two states in the reading. Go back to the map on pages 28–29. Color the two states the same color as you already colored Spain. (The map on pages 6–7 will help you find the states.) Remember that Spain also claimed Mexico. Color Mexico the same color as Spain.

UNDERSTANDING WHAT YOU READ: Comprehension Check

Read each statement. Write **T** for *True,* **F** for *False,* or **NG** if the information was *Not Given* in the story.

1. _____ Estevan was an Indian.

2. _____ The Spanish wanted to find gold.

3. _____ When Estevan was a prisoner in Texas, the Indians were cruel to him.

4. _____ Estevan could speak an Indian language.

5. _____ The Spanish sent an expedition to find the cities of gold.

6. _____ Fray Marcos and Estevan were good friends.

7. _____ Fray Marcos and Estevan led the expedition to New Mexico and Arizona.

8. _____ Fray Marcos was with Estevan when the Indians killed him.

9. _____ Estevan thought he had found one of the seven golden cities.

10. _____ Later explorers found the cities of gold.

WHAT DO YOU THINK?

Estevan was a slave. With one or more friends, discuss what this means. What is slavery? How was a slave different from other workers? How did a person become a slave? What countries used to have slaves? Are there any slaves today? Use an encyclopedia to help you answer these questions.

MAP SKILLS: Some Spanish Claims in North America

In the United States, some states have names given them by the Spanish explorers. Look at these names of states explored or settled by people from Spain and Mexico.

California (The name of an imaginary island in a Spanish book.)
Colorado (A Spanish word for red. The rocks and soil in parts of Colorado are red.)
Florida (From *Pascua Florida,* Spanish for Easter Sunday, the day in 1513 when it was named.)
Montana (From *montaña,* the Spanish word for mountain.)
Nevada (The Spanish word meaning snowy or covered with snow.)
New Mexico (From the Spanish name, *Nuevo Mejico.* Mexico is named for the Aztec war god, Mexitli.)
Texas (From *Tejas,* an Indian word meaning friends or allies.)

Color these seven states on the map. Then answer the questions. Use the large map of the United States on pages 6 and 7 to help you.

1. Which state is in the southeastern part of the U.S.? _____

2. Which state has a coast on the Pacific Ocean? _____

3. Which state has a coast on the Atlantic Ocean? _____

4. Which two states have a coast on the Gulf of Mexico? _____

5. Which four states do not touch any coast? _____

6. Which three states have borders with Mexico? _____

7. Which state has a border with Canada? _____

8. Which state is on the east border of California? _____

9. Which state is on the north border of New Mexico? _____

10. Do you live in one of these states with a Spanish name? _____

   If so, which one is it? _____

   If not, which of these states is nearest to where you live? _____

Now color these seven states on the map on pages 28–29. Remember to use the same color that you used for Spain.

Colorado

Texas

Montana

ACTIVITY: Investigating Names

With one or more friends, talk about the names of the countries, states or provinces, and cities that you come from. Use an encyclopedia or ask older family members or friends if you need to. What do the names mean? Who gave the places these names? Have the places always had these names, or were they called something else earlier? You may also want to find out about the names of the state and city you live in now.

Developing Reports: Spanish Explorers in North America

You are going to learn about some other Spanish explorers. You are going to follow five steps that will help you make better reports:

1. Read and study a report about one explorer.

2. Read and study a fact sheet about another explorer.

3. Write a report from the fact sheet.

4. Present your report orally to your classmates.

5. Listen and take notes on reports that your classmates present.

Step 1: Reading a Report

Read this report on the early Spanish explorer Cabeza de Vaca. Notice how the information is organized into an *introduction,* a *body,* and a *conclusion.*

Cabeza de Vaca

Introduction
Tells what the report is about.

This report is about Alvar Nuñez Cabeza de Vaca. He was a Spanish explorer. He was born about 1490, and he died about 1557. He explored parts of what are now the states of Florida and Texas. He claimed these areas for Spain.

Body
Tells the main adventures and gives details.

The first important point about Cabeza de Vaca is that he went to Florida in 1528 to look for gold. The black slave Estevan was a member of this expedition. The expedition got lost, and many men died. They did not find any gold, either. When Cabeza de Vaca finally got back to the coast where he had left his ships, the ships were gone!

The second important point is that Cabeza de Vaca and his men built small boats and tried to sail back to Mexico. A terrible storm sank most of the boats. A few boats landed on a small island near the coast of Texas. Cabeza de Vaca was in one of these boats. So was Estevan.

The third important point is that a group of Indians took Cabeza de Vaca and his men prisoners. While they were prisoners, Cabeza de Vaca and Estevan heard the Indians tell stories about seven cities of gold.

The fourth important point is that Cabeza de Vaca and his men were finally freed. They returned to Mexico City in 1536, eight years after they had left. They told about the cities of gold. The Spanish government sent more explorers to find these cities of gold.

Conclusion
Tells what the report was about and why Cabeza de Vaca was important.

In conclusion, this report has been about the Spanish explorer Cabeza de Vaca. He was important because he was one of the first explorers in Florida and Texas. Although he didn't find any gold, he did claim these areas for Spain. He also convinced the Spanish government that more explorers should be sent to look for gold.

Step 2: Studying a Fact Sheet

Now you will learn about two more explorers. You will work with a friend. Look at the fact sheets below. Each fact sheet has a time line of the explorer's life. Each tells you important things that the explorer did. Each also has a map showing where the explorer went.

- Decide which explorer each of you will report on. You will report on one of them, your friend will report on the other.

- Write your report on the next page. Use the fact sheet to help you.

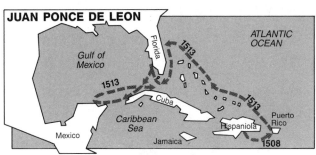

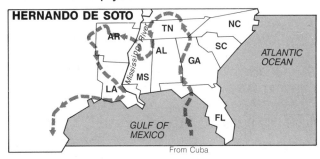

JUAN PONCE DE LEÓN		
	1474	Born in Spain.
1st important fact	1493	Sailed with Christopher Columbus on Columbus's second voyage to America. Settled in Hispaniola.
2nd important fact	1508	Explored Puerto Rico. Found gold there. Conquered Indians and claimed Puerto Rico for Spain. Became first governor of Puerto Rico (1509–1512). Heard stories about Fountain of Youth. "People who drink water of Fountain of Youth stay young forever."
3rd important fact	1513	Went in search of Fountain of Youth. Explored east coast and southern tip of Florida. (First European expedition to Florida.) Claimed land for Spain but didn't find Fountain of Youth.
4th important fact	1521	Second voyage to look for Fountain of Youth. Landed on west coast of Florida. Tried to start a colony. Indians attacked; Ponce de León killed.

HERNANDO DE SOTO		
	1500	Born in Spain.
1st important fact	1533	Went to Peru to help Spanish army conquer the Incas. Convinced Inca ruler to meet with Spanish commander; Spanish soldiers then captured Inca ruler.
2nd important fact	1538	Became governor of Cuba.
3rd important fact	1539	Decided to explore Florida, "a land of gold." Landed on west coast of Florida. Didn't find gold. Traveled throughout southeast section of North America looking for gold (1539–1541). Didn't find gold but claimed all land for Spain.
4th important fact	1541	Crossed the Mississippi River (first European to do so). Explored what are now Arkansas and Louisiana. Didn't find any gold. Returned to Mississippi River. Died of fever (1542). Buried in Mississippi River.

STEP 3: Writing a Report

TITLE OF REPORT _____

_____

Introduction   This report is about _____ .

He was a _____ explorer. He was born in _____ and he died in

_____ . He explored _____

_____ and he claimed these areas for _____ .

Body of Report   The first important point about _____
Tells the main
adventures of   _____
the explorer
and gives dates   _____
and some
details.   _____

The second important _____

_____

_____

_____

The third _____

_____

_____

_____

The fourth _____

_____

_____

Conclusion   In conclusion, this report has been about _____

_____ . He was important because

_____

STEP 4: Presenting a Report

Read over your report, and correct it as carefully as you can. Then practice reading it aloud at least five times. Read to a friend, to someone in your family, or make a tape recording and play it back. Check these things:

- Do I read too fast, too slow, or about right?

- Is my voice too loud, too soft, or about right?

- Is my pronunciation clear enough so that others understand me?

Next, practice using a map to show where your explorer went. If there is a big map in your classroom, you may wish to use it. You may also use the map of the United States on pages 6 and 7 of this book. Practice talking and pointing to the map at the same time. As you name each place your explorer went, point to it on the map.

When you feel ready, present your report to your partner. Your partner will take notes. Your partner may ask you questions, too.

STEP 5: Listening and Taking Notes

Listen to your partner's report and take notes on it. When you listen to a report, listen for the most important facts and dates. If you don't understand something, ask a question or ask to hear it again. Use the space below to take notes on your partner's report.

Name of Explorer _____ **Born** _____

Places explored (and other facts about the explorer)   **Dates**

_____   _____

_____   _____

_____   _____

_____   _____

_____   _____

_____   _____

_____   _____

UNDERSTANDING WHAT YOU READ: Using Maps

Now, go back to the map on pages 28–29 and color the areas that Cabeza de Vaca, Ponce De León, and De Soto claimed for Spain.

Explorers For England, France, and the Netherlands

BEFORE YOU READ: Vocabulary

bay: part of a sea or lake	**gulf:** a large bay

BEFORE YOU READ: Using Section Headings

Before you read the paragraphs, look at the title and the headings above each section. Then answer these questions.

1. What part of the Americas is this story about? _____

2. How many explorers does it tell about? _____

Now read the story to find out the details.

European Explorers in North America

Other Countries Send Explorers

Spain was the first European country to explore and establish colonies in the Americas—the New World. People in other European countries learned about the New World. These European countries sent explorers to find out about the new land. Later they sent colonists to settle in the new areas.

John Cabot

John Cabot came from Italy, but he explored for England. The King of England sent Cabot to North America in 1497. At this time, people in Europe still thought there was a sea route to the Indies across the Atlantic. They called this route the Northwest Passage. They thought it was north of the lands that Columbus found. Cabot looked for the Northwest Passage. He landed in what is now Newfoundland in Canada. Cabot's voyage was important because he claimed part of Canada for England.

Two Early French Explorers

Two early French explorers made trips to America for France. First was Jacques Cartier. He sailed in 1534 to look for the Northwest Passage. He reached the Gulf of St. Lawrence in Canada on this trip. On his second trip in 1535 he sailed up the St. Lawrence River. He called this area New France. His trips were important because he claimed all the land along the St. Lawrence River for France.

A second important French explorer was Samuel de Champlain. Champlain explored the coast of New France in 1608. He was important because he established the first French colony in America—Quebec.

Henry Hudson

An important English explorer was Henry Hudson. His first trip was not for England but for the Netherlands. In 1609 Hudson explored the coast of North America for the Dutch (the people of the Netherlands). He found a large river and sailed up it. Today we call this river the Hudson River. Hudson claimed all the land along this river for the Netherlands. This was important because Dutch colonists settled there later.

In 1610 Hudson made another trip. This time it was for England. He explored an area far in the north of what is now Canada. This trip was important because Hudson found a huge bay. He claimed all the land around it for England. Today this bay is called Hudson Bay.

European Territories in North America

Cabot, Cartier, Champlain, and Hudson were important because they explored parts of North America and claimed these lands for three different European countries—England, France, and the Netherlands. Spain was no longer the only European nation that claimed territory in North America.

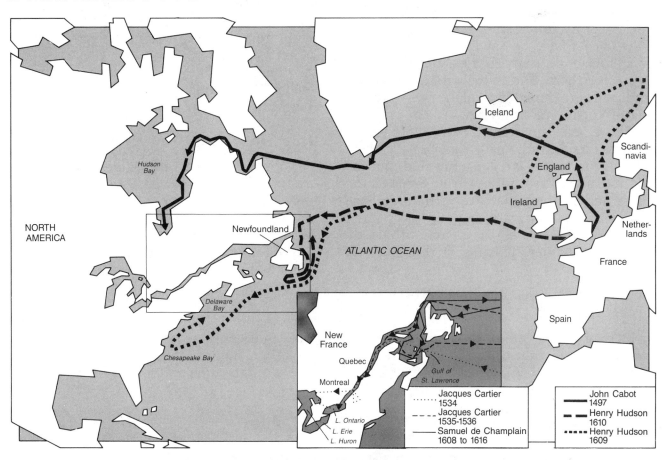

UNDERSTANDING WHAT YOU READ: Scanning and Taking Notes

Now scan the paragraphs. To *scan* means to read quickly to find important facts. Write the missing information in the chart below as you read. After you have filled in the chart, compare your notes with a classmate.

EXPLORER'S NAME	NATIONALITY	SPONSORING COUNTRY	DATE(S)	AREA EXPLORED	IMPORTANCE
Cabot					
Cartier					
Champlain					
Hudson					

UNDERSTANDING WHAT YOU READ: Using Maps

On the map on pages 28–29 color the areas explored by Cabot, Cartier, Champlain, and Hudson the same colors as the countries that claimed these areas.

Regions of the World: The Northern Forest Regions

What Are the Northern Forest Regions?

When Jacques Cartier reached the Gulf of the St. Lawrence and sailed up the St. Lawrence River, he saw land covered with thick forests of evergreen trees. He was exploring a Northern Forest Region. Champlain's and Hudson's Canadian explorations were also in the Northern Forest Region.

There are Northern Forest Regions in Europe, Asia, and North America. In these regions the winters are long and cold, but the summers are often quite warm. Some of the birds and animals that live in the Northern Forest Regions migrate south in the winter. Other animals, such as bears, hibernate during the winter. This means they sleep all winter.

Where Do People Live in the Northern Forest Regions?

Most of the people in the Northern Forest Regions live near the coast. This is because the winters are not so cold near the ocean. In the summer, the ocean becomes warm. It cools off very slowly, so the ocean is warmer than the land during the winter. During the winter, the wind from the ocean warms the land near the coast. Far away from the ocean in the Northern Forest Regions, the winters are much colder. Few people live inland in the Northern Forest Regions.

How Do the People Make a Living?

Many important natural resources come from the Northern Forest Regions. Important minerals such as iron ore, nickel, copper, and uranium come from the mines of Canada. Valuable wood comes from the northern forests of Finland. The Soviet Union sells the furs of animals that live in the forests of the north.

Some of the people in the Northern Forest Regions live and work in cities. Other people work in mines. People are needed to cut down trees and transport the wood. Some people make a living by trapping animals such as minks and beavers and selling their fur.

UNDERSTANDING WHAT YOU READ: Using Context

First, find and underline these eight words and phrases in the paragraphs above. Read the words that come just before and after in the story. This will help you guess the meaning of each new word. Then find the definition that matches the word. Write the letter of the definition on the line. Use a dictionary or the glossary if you need more help.

1. evergreen_____   a. To work and earn money.

2. fur_____   b. Materials such as wood and oil found on or in the earth and used by people.

3. hibernate_____   c. The soft hair of an animal.

4. make a living_____   d. To spend the winter asleep.

5. mine_____   e. Part of a tree that can be used for building a house.

6. natural resources_____   f. A kind of tree that keeps its leaves all year.

7. inland_____   g. A hole made to take things out of the earth such as coal or gold.

8. wood_____   h. Far away from the coast.

UNDERSTANDING BAR GRAPHS: Temperatures in the Northern Forest Region

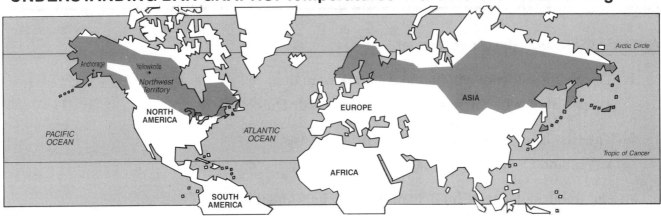

Yellowknife, Northwest Territories, Canada, and Anchorage, Alaska, U.S.A., are two cities in the Northern Forest Region. Find the cities on the map. The bar graphs show the year-round temperature in Yellowknife and Anchorage.

Yellowknife, NWT, Canada

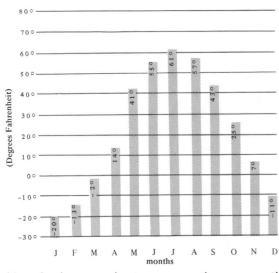

Anchorage, AK, U.S.A.

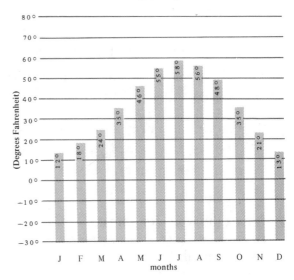

Use the bar graphs to answer these questions.

1. What is the warmest month in Yellowknife?_____ What is the temperature?_____

2. What is the warmest month in Anchorage?_____ What is the temperature?_____

3. What is the coldest month in Yellowknife?_____ What is the temperature?_____

4. What is the coldest month in Anchorage?_____ What is the temperature?_____

5. Circle the statements that are true:

    a. In both cities, the winter is much colder than the summer.

    b. The summer temperature is about the same in both cities.

    c. The winter temperature is about the same in both cities.

6. How is the weather different in these cities?_____

_____

Why? (Look at the reading on page 46.)_____

Exploration of the New World **47**

A. Circle the letter of the correct answer.

1. The first Europeans who found America were the:

   a. Spanish   **b.** Vikings   **c.** English   **d.** Dutch

2. The first European colony in North America was:

   a. Vinland   **b.** Hispaniola   **c.** Mexico City   **d.** Quebec

3. Columbus sailed west from Spain because he wanted to:

   a. discover America   b. find a better route to the Indies   **c.** find gold
   d. establish a new colony

4. Columbus reached America in the year:

   a. 1001   **b.** 1451   **c.** 1539   **d.** 1492

5. Estevan was important because he:

   a. discovered Florida   **b.** explored Texas, New Mexico, and Arizona
   c. crossed the Mississippi   **d.** established a colony

6. Estevan and Fray Marcos were looking for:

   a. the Northwest Passage   **b.** Mexico City   **c.** the seven cities of gold
   d. the Fountain of Youth

B. Check the words or phrases.

1. Check all the words or phrases that are related to the Wet Tropical Regions.

   ____warm   ____snowy   ____tundra   ____Tropic of Capricorn

   ____sugar cane   ____dry   ____Cuba   ____Puerto Rico

   ____hibernate   ____coffee   ____Antarctica   ____midnight sun

   ____rainy   ____igloos   ____Hispaniola   ____Tropic of Cancer

   ____plantations   ____equator   ____Hudson Bay   ____Maine

2. Check all the phrases that are related to the Northern Forest Regions.

   ____thick forests   ____near the equator

   ____cold winters   ____people mostly live near the coast

   ____bananas and coconuts   ____mineral and forest resources

   ____evergreen trees   ____Hudson Bay

   ____valuable animal furs   ____Mexico

   ____same temperature all year round   ____Canada

   ____south of Arctic Region   ____St. Lawrence River

C. Write your answers.

1. Write the name of four states in the United States that were first explored or settled by people from Spain and Mexico. (The states were named by these people.)

   _____ _____ _____ _____

2. For each country, name one explorer and tell what part of North America he explored.

   England_____

   France_____

   Spain_____

   The Netherlands_____

D. Use the words below to label the map.

Equator   Tropic of Cancer   Tropic of Capricorn   Africa   Europe
           Atlantic Ocean   Pacific Ocean

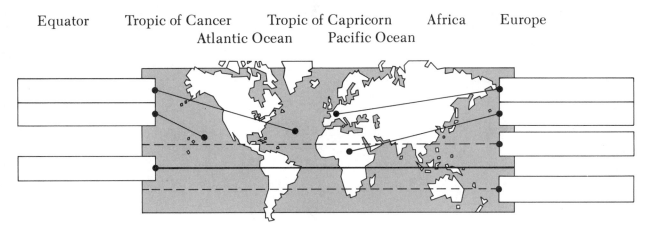

E. What Do You Think? Discuss these questions with a friend, a small group, or the class.

1. Why did European rulers pay people to explore North America?
2. Why did the explorers and rulers believe they could claim the land for their countries?
3. How do you think the Native Americans felt when Europeans claimed their land?

F. Role-Play

Imagine you are in Spain, in the royal palace, almost 500 years ago. Write two conversations that might have taken place between Columbus and Queen Isabella. Work with a small group of friends. After you have written and practiced the two conversations, people in your group can perform these short plays for the class.

1. It is 1492. Columbus is trying to convince Queen Isabella to give him money for his voyage.
2. It is 1493. Columbus has returned from his first voyage. He tells Queen Isabella about his discoveries. He convinces her to give him more money for another voyage.

Exploration of the New World   **49**

Colonies in the New World

In this unit you will:

- learn about the early Spanish colonies
- learn about the early English colonies and the first Thanksgiving
- read about the Mid-Latitude Forests
- use bar graphs and maps
- sharpen your listening, reporting and note-taking skills

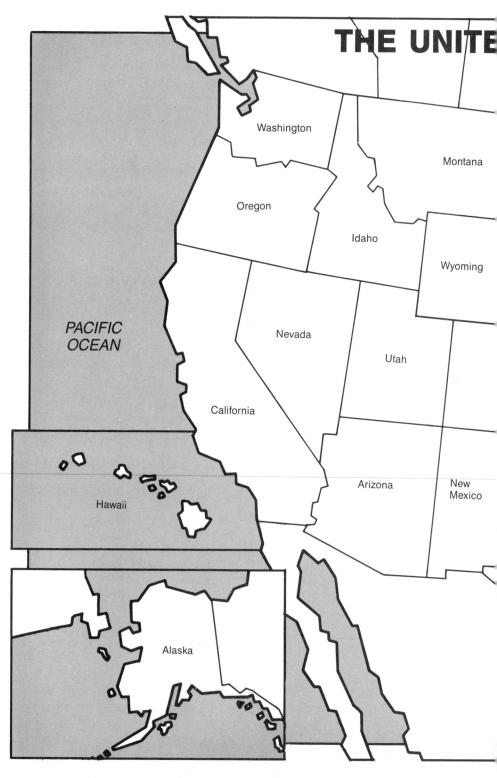

THE UNITE

Washington

Montana

Oregon

Idaho

Wyoming

PACIFIC
OCEAN

Nevada

Utah

California

Arizona

New
Mexico

Hawaii

Alaska

Where were the first colonies established?

What were the colonies like?

How were the colonies ruled?

Unit 3

Many of the early European colonies later became states. This map shows the United States and part of Canada today. As you read about the colonies established by Spain, England, France, and the Netherlands, find those states or areas on this map. Use the color key on this map to color in those states or areas.

Unit Map

• Fill in the color key for this map now.

• Use the same color for each European country as you did on the map on page 29.

STATES AND SOUTHERN CANADA

North Dakota

Minnesota

Maine

Michigan

Vermont

New Hampshire

Wisconsin

New York

Massachusetts

Rhode Island

South Dakota

Connecticut

Pennsylvania

New Jersey

Iowa

Washington, DC

Delaware

Maryland

Nebraska

Ohio

West Virginia

Virginia

Indiana

Illinois

Colorado

Kansas

Missouri

Kentucky

North Carolina

Tennessee

ATLANTIC OCEAN

Oklahoma

Arkansas

South Carolina

Mississippi River

Mississippi

Georgia

Alabama

Louisiana

Texas

Florida

St. Lawrence River

Hudson River

MEXICO

☐ Spanish Colonies
☐ English Colonies
☐ French Colonies
☐ Dutch Colonies (Netherlands)

Commonwealth of Puerto Rico

Spain in the New World

BEFORE YOU READ: Using Section Headings

There are four section headings in the reading, "Spanish Colonies."

A. Spanish Territories in the New World

C. Slaves are Brought to the Colonies

B. Colonies and Missions in North America

D. U.S. Cities with Spanish History

Under which heading would you look to find the answers to the following questions? Write the letter of the section heading on the line.

1. What is a mission? _____

2. What land did Spain own in the New World? _____

3. Was the city of Santa Fe, New Mexico, a Spanish colony? _____

4. Why did Spanish colonists start to use slaves? _____

Spanish Colonies

Spanish Territories in the New World

Spain claimed large areas of America, and named these lands New Spain. New Spain covered much of South America and all of Central America and Mexico. New Spain also included large parts of what became the southern and western United States.

The Spanish found gold and silver in Mexico and Peru. They looked for gold in parts of what is now the United States but they never found very much.

Colonies and Missions in North America

The Spanish established colonies in various parts of what is now the United States. In these colonies, the Spanish way of life, the Spanish language, and the Christian religion became very important.

Spanish priests taught the Native Americans about the Christian religion. In many places they set up missions. A mission was a church and the houses around it.

When Indians (Native Americans) came to live at the Spanish missions, they learned to speak, read, and write Spanish. They also learned about the Christian religion. The Indians worked hard at the missions. The Spanish would not allow the Indian workers to leave.

Slaves Are Brought to the Colonies

The Spanish needed more people in their colonies to build their cities and work on their farms. The Indians worked very hard, but the Spanish often treated them badly. Many of the Indians got sick and died. The Spanish decided to bring slaves from Africa to work for them at the missions and in the colonies of New Spain.

U.S. Cities with Spanish History

Many cities in the United States have Spanish names because they used to be Spanish colonies or missions. For example, San Juan, Puerto Rico, was founded and settled by the Spanish in 1521. It is the oldest city in the United States. In 1565, the Spanish founded St. Augustine, Florida. In 1610, they established another colony in Santa Fe, New Mexico.

The Spanish also settled in Texas. In 1682, a mission was established in El Paso. Another mission was set up in San Antonio, Texas, in 1720.

The Spanish set up colonies in California last. The first Spanish mission was established at San Diego, in 1769. Later, Spanish priests and settlers established many other missions in California.

UNDERSTANDING WHAT YOU READ: Comprehension Check

Read each statement. Write **T** for *True*, **F** for *False*, or **NG** if the information
was *Not Given* in the story.

1. _____ New Spain covered all of South America.

2. _____ The Spanish found gold and silver in Central and South America.

3. _____ The Spanish found a lot of gold in what is now the United States.

4. _____ There were more Spanish colonies in what is now the United States than there
   were in Central America.

5. _____ The Spanish wanted the Indians to become Christians.

6. _____ Spanish priests taught Indians reading, writing, and religion.

7. _____ African slaves were brought to the Spanish missions.

8. _____ The first city founded in what is today the United States was St. Augustine,
   Florida.

9. _____ The missions at El Paso and San Antonio were founded in the same year.

10. _____ Spanish colonies in California were established before the colonies in
    New Mexico.

UNDERSTANDING WHAT YOU READ: Scanning and Using Maps

When you scan a reading, you look quickly through it to find certain things. Scan the reading
on page 52. Look for the names of four states in which the Spanish established missions and
colonies. Write the names of the states below.

_____   _____   _____   _____

Now find and color these states on the map on page 51.

England in the New World

BEFORE YOU READ: Vocabulary

You will need to understand the words in this crossword puzzle as you read about the English colonies. The vocabulary words are listed in the Word Box at the bottom of this page. Fill in the crossword puzzle. Use a dictionary or the glossary if you need help.

ACROSS

3. Lasting forever (or a very long time).
4. To build homes and live in a new area.
5. To think the same thing.
8. A big meal with special food.
9. To pick or gather crops when they are ready to eat.
11. Government by the people.
13. People smoke the leaves of this plant in cigarettes and pipes.
15. The part of the year after winter and before summer.

DOWN

1. Rules set by the government that people must follow.
2. Chose.
6. The people or the system that rule a country, city, etc.
7. More than half the total number of people.
8. Human rights; the opposite of slavery.
10. Having the same rights.
12. A group of people who help govern, make laws, etc.
14. Plants grown for food or money.

WORD BOX			
agree	equal	harvest	selected
council	feast	laws	settle
crop	freedom	majority	spring
democracy	government	permanent	tobacco

The First English Colonies

Why Were the Colonies Established?

In the late 1500s and early 1600s, English colonies were established in North America. Some colonies were established because people wanted to find gold. Other colonies were established because people wanted to be free to have their own religion.

The Roanoke Island Colony

The first English colony in America was established in 1588 on Roanoke Island, off the coast of North Carolina. Two years later, a ship from England arrived at Roanoke Island, bringing the colonists food, clothes, and other supplies. But the colony was no longer there! All the colonists had disappeared. No one ever found out what happened to them.

The Jamestown Colony

The first permanent English colony was at Jamestown, Virginia. This colony was established in 1607. At first the colonists had many problems. The land was not good for farming, and the colonists were more interested in finding gold than in farming. During the first winter many of the colonists got sick and died.

Then Captain John Smith became the leader of the Jamestown colony. He organized the colony and told people to build houses and to plant crops. Eventually the colonists began to grow tobacco and sell it to the people in England. The colonists of Jamestown made good money from their tobacco crop.

At first, the Jamestown colonists had problems getting along with the Native Americans. A story told by Captain John Smith shows this. He said that an Indian Chief captured him. The chief wanted to kill Captain Smith, but the chief's daughter, Pocahontas, asked her father to let John Smith live, so his life was saved. Nobody knows if the story is true, but Pocahontas was a real person, and she later married an Englishman and went to live in London.

After a while, the Jamestown colonists and the Indians became more friendly, and they began to trade.

In 1619, the people of Jamestown selected a small group of colonists, which they called a council, to make laws. The council's job was to govern the colony. This meant that the colonists of Jamestown had some freedom to decide for themselves how they wanted to live.

The Jamestown colony was important for two major reasons. It was the first permanent English colony in America, and it was the start of democratic government in America.

Captain John Smith

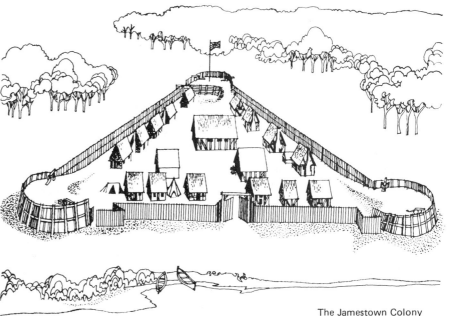

The Jamestown Colony

The Plymouth Colony

The second permanent English colony was founded in Massachusetts by a group of people called the Pilgrims or Separatists. The Pilgrims wanted the freedom to follow their own religion. They did not have this freedom in England. So they decided to travel to America and establish a colony there.

On a fall day in 1620, the Pilgrims sailed from Plymouth, England, in a small ship called the *Mayflower*. They planned to land near the mouth of the Hudson River in North America.

A big storm blew the small ship far north of the Hudson River. In November, 1620, it landed on Cape Cod in Massachusetts. The weather was too bad for the *Mayflower* to sail down the coast. Instead, the captain and some men looked for a good place to spend the winter. They decided on a nearby harbor. The map told them that the harbor was called Plymouth. It was named after the English town from which the Pilgrims had sailed!

The Pilgrims wrote an agreement. This agreement was called the *Mayflower Compact*. The *Mayflower Compact* said that the people in Plymouth Colony would live under one government. The Pilgrims would make their own laws and everyone would have to obey these laws. Forty-one men signed the *Mayflower Compact*.

The Pilgrims of Plymouth Colony had many problems. In the first winter, half of the Pilgrims died. But in the spring, the ones that were left worked hard to build houses and plant crops.

The Wampanoag Indians lived in the area around Plymouth Colony. The chief of the Wampanoags was a man called Massasoit. The Wampanoag were friendly and taught the Pilgrims how to plant corn and make maple syrup. The Pilgrims planted corn, squash, and beans. In the fall, they had a good harvest.

The Pilgrims had a feast in the fall of 1621 to celebrate their first harvest. They invited Massasoit and their other Wampanoag friends to the feast. We remember this harvest feast each November in the United States when we celebrate Thanksgiving Day.

The Plymouth colony was important for three major reasons. It was the first colony that was established because people wanted religious freedom. A second important reason was that the Pilgrims wrote the *Mayflower Compact* and agreed to live under one government. This was a step towards a democratic government. The third reason is that the Pilgrims' harvest feast is remembered by Americans each year as they celebrate Thanksgiving.

In conclusion, Jamestown and Plymouth were the first two permanent English colonies in America. Some very important ideas in American democracy started in these two colonies.

UNDERSTANDING WHAT YOU READ: Scanning and Taking Notes

Scan the paragraphs about Jamestown and Plymouth to find the missing information for the chart on this page. Remember that when you scan, you read quickly to find certain facts or other pieces of information. Use the chart to take notes on what you find. You do not need to write complete sentences. Just write the important words.

	JAMESTOWN	PLYMOUTH
1. Year established		
2. The first winter: problems		
3. Farming: solving the problems, main crops		
4. The Indians and the colonists		
5. Type of government		
6. Importance of colony		

UNDERSTANDING WHAT YOU READ: Comparing and Contrasting

With one or more friends, discuss the information on the chart. Compare and contrast the two colonies. When you compare things, you think about ways that they are the same. When you contrast things, you think about the ways they are different.

UNDERSTANDING WHAT YOU READ: Using Maps

In what state was the Jamestown colony? In what state was the Plymouth colony? People of what country established these two colonies? Find the two states on the map on page 51 and color them with the color for that country.

Colonies in the New World   **57**

Life in Plymouth Colony, 1627

ACTIVITY: Discussing and Interpreting Photographs

The photographs on this page come from Plimoth Plantation, a "living museum" in Massachusetts. At Plimoth Plantation you can see people living the way the colonists did in 1627.

Talk about these pictures with your classmates. What are the people in the photographs doing? What tools are they using? What other things do you see? What do these photographs tell you about life in Plymouth Colony?

Thanksgiving

Thanksgiving is an important holiday in the United States. It is celebrated every year on the fourth Thursday of November. American families, and often friends, get together to celebrate. An important part of this celebration is the Thanksgiving dinner. This feast includes some of the foods that were served at the first Thanksgiving. It includes other foods that have been served at Thanksgiving for many, many years. Many families also have their own special Thanksgiving foods.

At the first Thanksgiving, the Pilgrims gave thanks for their good harvest and for their friendship with the Indians. Nowadays, we also give thanks for good food and good friends.

"The First Thanksgiving" by Jennie Brownscomb

Look at the two menus below. One menu lists what the Pilgrims probably ate at their Thanksgiving. The other menu lists what many Americans eat today for Thanksgiving.

Pilgrims' Thanksgiving Feast

deer	*clams*
roast duck	*bread*
roast goose	*wild plums*
roast turkey	*berries*

Today's Thanksgiving

roast stuffed turkey	*bread and butter*
cranberry sauce	*a dessert such as pumpkin*
sweet potatoes	*pie, apple pie,*
two or three vegetables	*or "Indian pudding"*

Does your family celebrate Thanksgiving? What do you have for dinner? Write the foods below.

_____

_____

Developing Reports: Family Recipes

Does anyone in your family have a special recipe for making any of the Thanksgiving foods listed on page 60? Please ask at home, and then bring the recipe to school. Or, if you like, bring a recipe for another food that is served at another special family celebration.

You will write and share your recipes by following four steps:

1. Read and study a Thanksgiving recipe.
2. Write your own family recipe, using the recipe you have studied as a model.
3. Present your recipe orally to a small group of classmates.
4. Take notes on the recipes that two of your classmates present.

Step 1: Studying a Recipe

Read the recipe below. Notice how the recipe is organized into *ingredients*—what you need—and *instructions*—how to make it.

Name of Recipe: *CRANBERRY SAUCE*

List of Ingredients

2 cups water	4 cups (1 pound) cranberries
2 cups sugar	2 teaspoons grated orange rind

Instructions

1. Wash the cranberries. Remove any bad berries.
2. Place the water and sugar in a saucepan. Stir until the sugar is dissolved.
3. Boil the water and sugar for 5 minutes.
4. Add the cranberries to the boiling sugar water.
5. Lower the heat. Gently simmer the cranberries for about 5 minutes, or until the sauce is very thick. Do not cover the saucepan. Do not stir.
6. Take off any foam from the cranberry sauce.
7. Add the grated orange rind. Stir it in.
8. Pour the cranberry sauce into dishes.
9. Put in the refrigerator to chill until the sauce is firm.

Step 2: Writing a Recipe

Now write your own recipe. First, write the name of the recipe and the name of the person who gave it to you. Then write the list of ingredients. Finally, write the instructions for making the recipe. Be sure to write the instructions in the right order. Each instruction should start with a verb that tells you what to do. For example: "*Clean* the vegetables. *Heat* the milk. *Bake* in a hot oven."

Write your recipe on the next page. Use more paper if you need to.

Name of My Recipe_____ Name of Person_____

List of Ingredients

_____ _____ _____

_____ _____ _____

_____ _____ _____

Instructions

1._____

2._____

3._____

4._____

5._____

6._____

7._____

8._____

STEP 3: Presenting Your Recipe

Before you present your recipe, practice reading it aloud at least five times. You can practice reading it to a friend or someone in your family, or you can make a tape recording and play it back. When you feel ready, present your recipe to your classmates. Remember to speak slowly and clearly so your classmates can take notes.

STEP 4: Listening to Recipes and Taking Notes

Now listen to two recipes from your classmates. Listen carefully and write down the ingredients and the key words of the instructions. If you don't understand a part of the recipe, ask questions. Write the two recipes on the lines below and on the next page.

Name of Recipe_____ Name of Person_____

List of Ingredients

_____ _____ _____

_____ _____ _____

_____ _____ _____

Instructions

1. _____
2. _____
3. _____
4. _____
5. _____
6. _____
7. _____
8. _____

Name of Recipe_____   **Name of Person**_____

List of Ingredients

_____   _____   _____

_____   _____   _____

_____   _____   _____

Instructions

1. _____
2. _____
3. _____
4. _____
5. _____
6. _____
7. _____
8. _____

Massasoit

LISTENING AND TAKING NOTES

You are going to listen to some information about Massasoit, the Native American chief who helped the Pilgrims. As you listen, take notes on the information using the T-List below. Remember, the *main ideas* are written on the left. You have to complete the *details* on the right.

MAIN IDEAS	DETAILS AND EXAMPLES
A. Who Massasoit was; what he did for Pilgrims	1. _____ of Wampanoag _____ . 2. Peace treaty with _____ in _____ .
B. First Thanksgiving	1. _____ friendly, helpful. 2. Pilgrims invited _____ to _____ .
C. Massasoit and Pilgrims helped each other	1. When Massasoit _____ Pilgrims helped him get well. 2. Massasoit _____ Pilgrims about _____ .
D. Problems after Massasoit's death	1. Son Metacomet (_____ Philip) attacked _____ . 2. War for _____ years. 3. Many _____, both sides.
E. Conclusion: Importance of Massasoit	1. Signed treaty with _____ . 2. Believed in _____ .

Writing a Report: Anne Hutchinson

Anne Hutchinson was a settler who came to the Massachusetts Bay Colony. The Massachusetts Bay Colony was another colony established by English people who wanted freedom to follow their own religion. These people were called Puritans, and they settled near Boston nine years after the Pilgrims established Plymouth colony. Anne Hutchinson liked to talk about religion. She was intelligent, and she thought that people should make their own decisions about what they believed. She had problems with the Puritan leaders because of her ideas. The leaders did not want anybody to have ideas that were different from their own.

Read the facts about the life of Anne Hutchinson below:

1. Born about 1591 in England.
2. To Massachusetts Bay Colony, 1634.
3. Settled in Boston.
4. Meetings with Boston women: talked about religion, Bible, Puritan laws.
5. Puritans did not like Hutchinson's ideas.
6. Tried by Puritan leaders.
7. Told to leave Massachusetts Bay Colony.
8. With husband to Rhode Island, 1638.
9. Husband died, 1642.
10. Moved to New Amsterdam (New York).
11. Died, 1643.

Look up information about Anne Hutchinson in an encyclopedia or textbook. Ask your teacher or school librarian to help you. Find at least one more fact about her life. Write the new fact here.

_____

_____

Next, read the facts about Anne Hutchinson's life again. Where does your new fact fit in? Draw a star to show where you want to add your new fact.

Finally, write a complete sentence (or two) about each fact in Anne Hutchinson's life. Be sure you write a sentence about your new fact, too. Write your sentences so that you have a complete paragraph about Anne Hutchinson. The first sentence is written for you. Use another sheet of paper for your paragraph.

Anne Hutchinson was born in England in about 1591.

_____

_____

_____

_____

_____

Regions of the World: The Mid-Latitude Forest Regions

When English colonists came to Jamestown and Plymouth and Massachusetts Bay, they found a region of great forests. This type of region is called the Mid-Latitude Forest. Latitudes are imaginary lines drawn around the world from east to west. Look at the map below. The equator, the Tropic of Cancer, the Tropic of Capricorn, the Arctic Circle, and the Antarctic Circle are all latitude lines. The Mid-Latitude Forests are located in the middle latitudes. They are between the Arctic Circle and the Tropic of Cancer and between the Antarctic Circle and the Tropic of Capricorn.

In Mid-Latitude Forest Regions there are seasons. The winters are cold or cool, and the summers are warm or hot. Most of the trees lose their leaves in the fall and grow new leaves in the spring. Some of the natural resources in these regions are coal and iron. The trees are another important natural resource. Lumber and wood products are made from them. There are many people. Almost half the people in the world live in Mid-Latitude Forest Regions.

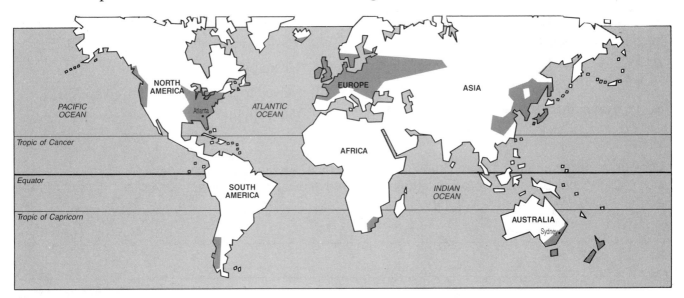

USING MAPS

Look at the map. Write short answers to the questions.

1. Which continents have Mid-Latitude Forest Regions? _____

    _____

2. Name two continents that have a narrow Mid-Latitude Forest Region along a coast.

    _____   _____

The equator is an imaginary line around the center of the earth. It is halfway between the North Pole and the South Pole. All the area north of the equator is called the northern hemisphere. All the area south of the equator is called the southern hemisphere.

3. Do you live in the northern hemisphere or the southern hemisphere? _____

4. Which hemisphere has more Mid-Latitude Forest Regions? _____

5. Do you live in a Mid-Latitude Forest Region? _____

UNDERSTANDING BAR GRAPHS: Temperatures in Mid-Latitude Forest Regions

The bar graphs on this page show the average monthly temperature in Atlanta, Georgia, U.S.A., and Sydney, New South Wales, Australia. Both cities are in Mid-Latitude Forest Regions. Find the two cities on the map on page 66. Remember that the letters at the bottom of each graph stand for the months of the year, starting with January. Use the bar graphs to answer these questions.

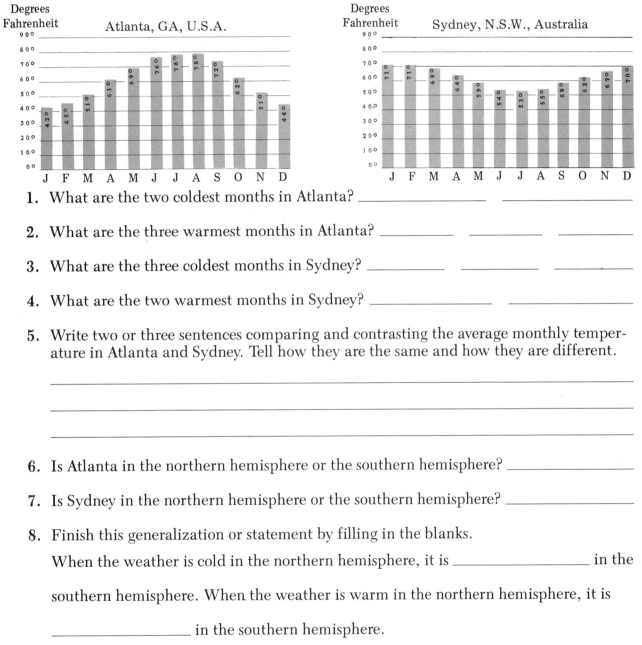

1. What are the two coldest months in Atlanta? _____ _____

2. What are the three warmest months in Atlanta? _____ _____ _____

3. What are the three coldest months in Sydney? _____ _____ _____

4. What are the two warmest months in Sydney? _____ _____

5. Write two or three sentences comparing and contrasting the average monthly temperature in Atlanta and Sydney. Tell how they are the same and how they are different.

_____

_____

_____

6. Is Atlanta in the northern hemisphere or the southern hemisphere? _____

7. Is Sydney in the northern hemisphere or the southern hemisphere? _____

8. Finish this generalization or statement by filling in the blanks.

   When the weather is cold in the northern hemisphere, it is _____ in the

   southern hemisphere. When the weather is warm in the northern hemisphere, it is

   _____ in the southern hemisphere.

WHAT DO YOU THINK?

One of the graphs shows a large difference between the temperature in the warmer months and the temperature in the colder months. The other graph shows a small difference. Discuss why the two graphs don't show the same amount of difference. Think about the locations of the two cities. (Hint: look back at pages 46 and 47 if you need to.)

The French and Dutch in North America

French Explorers and Colonies

France explored and claimed large areas of North America. The first French colony was Quebec, in what is today Canada.

The French also explored large parts of what is today the United States. In 1673, Marquette and Joliet, two French explorers, traveled along the upper part of the Mississippi River. They claimed the area they explored for France. Then in 1682, La Salle went all the way to the mouth of the Mississippi. (The *mouth* of a river is where it meets the ocean. Today, the city of New Orleans is near the mouth of the Mississippi.) La Salle claimed all the lands along the Mississippi River for France.

Most of the French people who came to North America were interested in trapping animals and selling the furs to people in Europe. The French trappers were friendly with the Indians. The Indians helped the French trappers catch the animals. The French were more interested in the fur trade than in establishing colonies in the New World.

Peter Minuit buys Manhattan.

Dutch Explorers and Colonies

The Dutch were also interested in furs from America. The Dutch explored and claimed the land along the Hudson River. This area is part of the state of New York today. Dutch fur trappers caught animals along the Hudson River and sold the furs to people in Europe.

In 1624, the Dutch governor, Peter Minuit, bought the island of Manhattan from the Indians. He paid for it with a chest full of beads, cloth, and tools worth less than $100. Manhattan is at the mouth of the Hudson River. The Dutch built a colony on Manhattan. They called their colony New Amsterdam. (Amsterdam is the capital of the Netherlands.)

In the mid-1600s, England and the Netherlands fought a war. The English won and took over the Dutch colony on Manhattan. They changed the name of the colony to New York.

By the end of the 1600s, only the Spanish, French, and English had colonies in North America.

French fur traders

UNDERSTANDING WHAT YOU READ: Comprehension Check

Complete the sentences below.

1. The name of the oldest French colony in America is _____ .

2. The French explorers who traveled along the northern part of the Mississippi River were _____ .

3. The area that La Salle explored was _____
   _____ .

4. The main reason the French came to America was _____
   _____ .

5. The French fur trappers had help from _____ .

6. The area of the Hudson River was claimed by _____ .

7. The Dutch paid the Indians for _____ .

8. The first name of New York was _____ .

9. The Dutch colony on Manhattan became English because _____
   _____ .

10. By 1700, the three European countries with colonies in North America were _____ .

UNDERSTANDING WHAT YOU READ: Using Maps

Remember to color in the areas claimed by France on the map (page 51).
Then color in the areas claimed by the Dutch. You may want to use the
colors for both the Netherlands and England on the areas claimed first
by the Dutch and then by the English.

New Amsterdam

Colonies in the New World   **69**

The Thirteen English Colonies

English Colonies in North America

Jamestown and Plymouth were the first permanent English colonies in North America. During the next 100 years, England established more colonies along the Atlantic coast. Finally, in the 1700s, there were thirteen English colonies in North America.

The thirteen English Colonies can be divided into three groups: the New England colonies, the Mid-Atlantic colonies, and the Southern colonies.

The New England Colonies

There were four New England colonies. These colonies were the farthest north on the Atlantic coast. The four New England colonies were Massachusetts, Rhode Island, Connecticut, and New Hampshire. What is now the state of Maine was part of the colony of Massachusetts. In this part of North America, the land was rocky and hard to farm. The fishing, however, was excellent. Many New England colonists became fishermen. The forests in New England were an excellent natural resource. Fish and wood, or lumber, became important products of the New England colonies.

The Mid-Atlantic Colonies

The four Mid-Atlantic colonies were New York, New Jersey, Pennsylvania, and Delaware. What is today Vermont was part of New York. Farming was good in the Mid-Atlantic colonies, and so farm products, especially wheat, became important here.

The Southern Colonies

The five Southern colonies were Virginia, Maryland, North Carolina, South Carolina, and Georgia. The land here was good, too, and the farms in the Southern colonies were very large. They were called plantations. Tobacco, rice, and cotton were grown on these plantations.

The Southern plantation owners needed many workers. They began to buy African slaves to work on their land. There were also

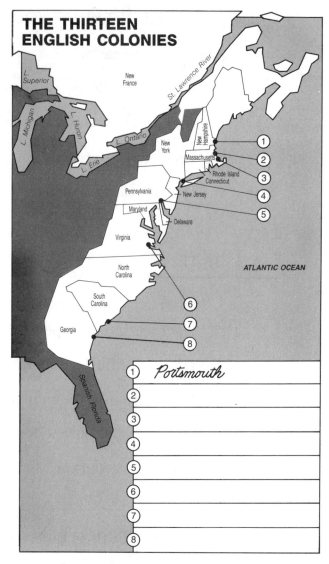

some African slaves in the other English colonies in the 1700s, but most of the slaves were on the plantations in the five Southern colonies.

England and the Thirteen Colonies

Most of the important cities in the thirteen colonies were ports. Ports are cities on the ocean (or a river or lake) where large ships can come and go.

Ships from Europe came to the American ports. They brought products from Europe such as cloth, tools, furniture, books, and tea. The ships took American products, such as wood, tobacco, cotton, and furs, back to Europe.

The king of England ruled the thirteen colonies. However, each colony also had its own government that helped make laws for that colony.

UNDERSTANDING WHAT YOU READ: Using Maps

1. Read "The Thirteen English Colonies" on page 70 again. Find and underline the names of the thirteen colonies. What country owned the thirteen colonies? On the map on page 51, color the areas of the thirteen colonies with the color of that country.

2. Now look at the map of the thirteen colonies on page 70. On this map, write the names of the following important colonial cities and towns. Use the large map of the United States on pages 6 and 7 to help you.

Portsmouth   *Philadelphia*
Jamestown   *Boston*
Charleston   *Plymouth*
New York City   *Savannah*
Portsmouth is done for you.

3. Compare these eight cities and towns. In what important way are they the same?

_____

_____

UNDERSTANDING WHAT YOU READ: Writing Study Questions

Write questions about the thirteen colonies. Begin your questions with *What, Where, How* and *Why.*

1. _____

    _____

2. _____

    _____

3. _____

    _____

4. _____

    _____

5. _____

    _____

6. _____

    _____

7. _____

    _____

8. _____

    _____

9. _____

    _____

10. _____

    _____

ACTIVITY: Study Quiz

Now work with two other students. Take turns asking one another your questions about the thirteen English colonies. Count 1 point for each correct answer. Write the scores in the boxes.

| Name _____ | Name _____ | Name _____ |
| Score _____ | Score _____ | Score _____ |

The French and Indian War: Before and After

BEFORE YOU READ: Using Maps

This map shows the areas that France, England, and Spain claimed in North America in 1750. Color each area the color you used for its country on the map on page 51. Notice that another European country also claimed land in North America in 1750. Russia claimed part of Alaska. Choose a color for Russia and color the Russian area. Remember to color the key, also.

1. Which country claimed the largest area?

   _____

   _____

2. Which countries claimed areas along the Atlantic Coast?

   _____

   _____

   _____

3. Which countries claimed parts of what is now Canada?

   _____

   _____

   _____

4. Which countries claimed areas along the Pacific Coast?

   _____

   _____

5. Which parts of today's United States were not claimed by any European country?

   _____

   _____

   _____

   _____

Key:
- Russia
- England
- France
- Spain

NORTH AMERICA BEFORE THE FRENCH AND INDIAN WAR

The French and Indian War

What Was the War About?

In 1754 a war broke out between France and England. Both the French and the English wanted the lands west of the Appalachian Mountains.

As you remember, French explorers had claimed all the land on both sides of the Mississippi River for France. But the English wanted to move west because the land between the Appalachian Mountains and the Mississippi was very good for farming. So there was war between France and England about who would own that land.

Who Fought in the War?

The war between France and England took place all over the world. Different countries and people joined the war. Some of them fought on the side of France. Others fought on the side of England. In America, some Indian tribes joined with the French to fight the English. Other Indian tribes joined with the English. Of course, the thirteen English colonies fought on the English side. One of the English leaders was Major George Washington, a young man from the colony of Virginia.

What Happened at the End of the War?

The war lasted for six years, from 1754 to 1760. Many people died on both sides. Finally the English won. They captured Quebec and Montreal, and the French surrendered.

At the end of the French and Indian War, the French had to give the English all the land east of the Mississippi River. Spain had to give England the territory of Florida. The French had to give the Spanish the lands west of the Mississippi River. They also had to give the

George Washington leads his soldiers.

Spanish the port of New Orleans. So the result of the French and Indian War was that England got much more territory in North America, and France lost all of its territory on the North American continent.

UNDERSTANDING WHAT YOU READ: Using Maps

Look at the map. It shows the results of the French and Indian War. Fill in the map key. Use the same colors as you did for the map on page 72. Next, color the map to show the territories claimed by England, France, and Spain at the end of the war.

1. Name five of today's states in the area France gave to England after this war.

_____

_____

_____

_____

2. What was the name of the territory that Spain had to give to England?

_____

3. What area was still claimed by France?

_____

Map: NORTH AMERICA AFTER THE FRENCH AND INDIAN WAR

Labels on map: Alaska, Hudson Bay, Newfoundland, Quebec, Montreal, Boston, New York, Atlantic Ocean, Louisiana, Santa Fe, New Mexico, Texas, San Antonio, Charleston, St. Augustine, New Orleans, Pacific Ocean, Gulf of Mexico, Guadeloupe, Cuba, Jamaica, Haiti, Puerto Rico, Martinique, New Spain, Mexico City, Caribbean Sea, Mississippi River

Map Key:
- Russia
- England
- France
- Spain

A. Circle the letter of the correct answer.

1. The Spanish established colonies in:
   a. Virginia, Massachusetts, and Connecticut   **b.** New York, Pennsylvania, and Virginia
   c. Texas, New Mexico, and California   **d.** Canada, New York, and Rhode Island

2. The first two permanent English colonies were:
   a. Jamestown and Plymouth   **b.** St. Augustine and Santa Fe   **c.** Quebec and New York
   d. Boston and Philadelphia

3. The first people to celebrate Thanksgiving were:
   a. Captain John Smith and Pocahontas   **b.** Spanish priests and African slaves
   c. French and Indian fur trappers   **d.** the Pilgrims and Massasoit's tribe

4. By 1700, the three European countries which had colonies in North America were:
   a. Spain, France, and England   **b.** the Netherlands, France, and England
   c. Spain, the Netherlands, and France   **d.** Spain, the Netherlands, and England

5. Anne Hutchinson was important because she:
   a. was married   **b.** believed in freedom of religion   **c.** was English
   d. lived in Boston, Rhode Island, and New Amsterdam

6. The European country that first settled the area that is today New York was:
   a. Spain   **b.** England   **c.** France   **d.** the Netherlands

7. The French and Indian War was fought between:
   a. France and American Indians   **b.** the United States and France
   c. England and France   **d.** American Indians and the United States

8. At the end of the French and Indian War, which country got more land in North America?
   a. Spain   **b.** France   **c.** Canada   **d.** England

B. Check the words or phrases.

1. Check all the words or phrases that are related to the Mid-Latitude Forest Regions.
   ____ northern hemisphere   ____ trees lose leaves   ____ lumber, coal, and iron
   ____ seasons   ____ few people   ____ southern hemisphere
   ____ polar climate   ____ hot, rainy climate   ____ tropical animals

2. Check all the words or phrases that are related to *democracy.*
   ____ Mayflower Compact   ____ laws decided by the people
   ____ government by the people   ____ slavery
   ____ king and queen   ____ Spanish missions
   ____ Jamestown council   ____ freedom

3. Which of the following states were among the thirteen English colonies?
   ____ Illinois   ____ Pennsylvania   ____ North Carolina   ____ Rhode Island
   ____ Virginia   ____ Georgia   ____ Mississippi   ____ New Jersey
   ____ Alabama   ____ California   ____ Massachusetts   ____ South Carolina
   ____ Texas   ____ New Hampshire   ____ Delaware   ____ Maine

C. This map shows the area that used to be the thirteen English colonies. There are now fifteen states in that area. Write the names of the fifteen states.

1. _____   8. _____

2. _____   9. _____

3. _____   10. _____

4. _____   11. _____

5. _____   12. _____

6. _____   13. _____

7. _____   14. _____

     15. _____

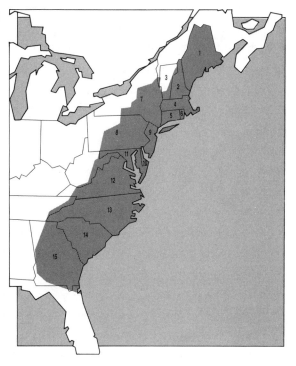

D. What Do You Think?

Discuss these questions with a friend, a small group, or the class. You may want to look up some information in the library.

1. Was the state you live in claimed by Europeans? If so, which country (or countries) claimed it?

2. In the early 1700s, how did the European people in your state live? What sort of houses did they build? How did they make a living? In what part of the state did they live? What sort of government did they have?

3. What Native American tribes lived in your state? What sort of houses did they build? What did they eat? What sort of government did they have? What happened to the tribes? Do many of these Native Americans still live in your state?

E. Role-Play

Imagine you are in Plymouth, Massachusetts in the fall of 1621. Write three conversations that might have taken place between the following people. Work with a small group of friends. Write enough parts in each conversation so everyone in your group has something to say. After your group has written and practiced the conversations, you can perform at least one of these short plays for the class.

1. You are Pilgrims at Plymouth Colony. You have just had a very good harvest. Plan the first Thanksgiving celebration.

2. You are members of the Wampanoag tribe. The colonists of Plymouth have invited you to a Thanksgiving celebration. Do you want to go? Discuss what you are going to bring to the feast.

3. Some of you are Pilgrims and some of you are Wampanoags. You are having a Thanksgiving feast together. What do you talk about?

A New Nation

DELAWARE.

PENNSYLVANIA.

NEW JERSEY.

GEORGIA.

CONNECTICUT.

MASSACHUSETTS.

MARYLAND.

SOUTH CAROLINA

VIRGINIA.

NEW YORK.

NEW HAMPSHIRE.   **NORTH CAROLINA.**   **RHODE ISLAND.**

In this unit you will:

- read about the Stamp Act and the Boston Tea Party
- learn about the American Revolution
- learn about the Declaration of Independence
- learn about the American government
- use maps, make time lines and line graphs
- sharpen your writing and reporting skills
- sharpen your listening and note-taking skills

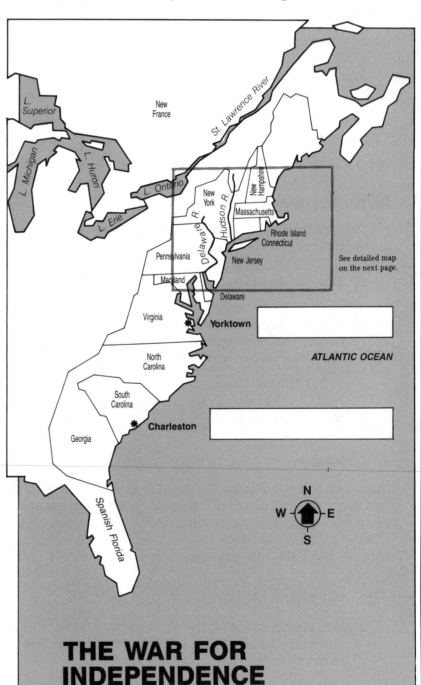

THE WAR FOR INDEPENDENCE

Why were the thirteen colonies unhappy with British rule?

What did they do about it?

What was the result?

Unit 4

The maps on these pages show the thirteen English colonies at the time of the War for Independence. Some important battles in this war are marked on the maps with this symbol (✱). As you read about what happened at each of these battles, look at the maps to find out where the battles were and write the month and year of each battle.

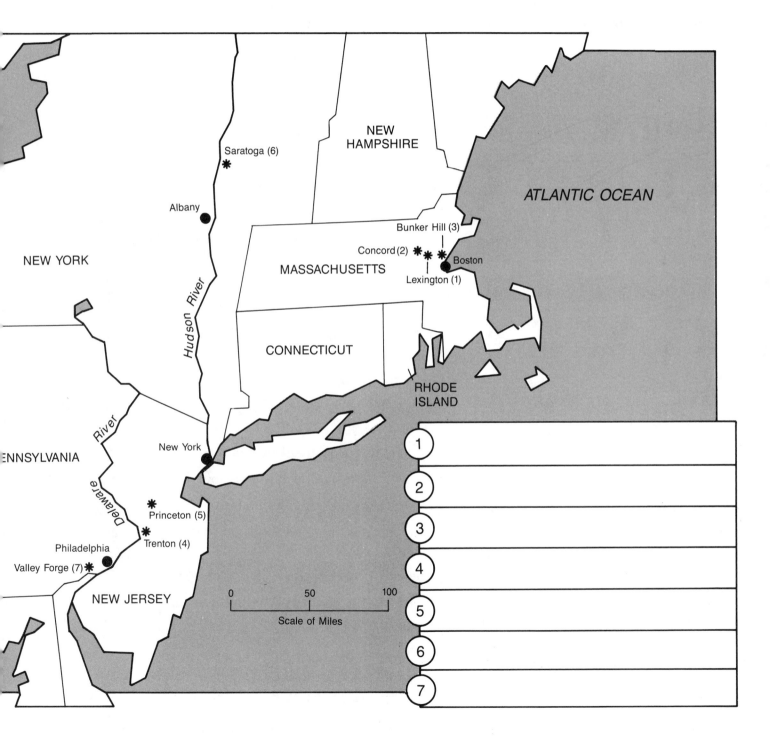

The Colonies Begin to Dislike British Rule

BEFORE YOU READ: Vocabulary

allow	fire (a gun)	intolerable	pass (a law)	repeal	rule
British	import	massacre	protest	representative	ruler
cargo	independent	Parliament	provide	rights	tax

Write each word next to its definition. Use a dictionary or the glossary at the end of this book if you need to. Check your answers with a friend.

1. _____ A load of goods or products that is carried on a ship, truck, train, or airplane.

2. _____ To bring goods or products into a country.

3. _____ Too much to endure; more than one can bear or put up with.

4. _____ Words or an action that show that a person is against something.

5. _____ Things that the law allows people to do or have.

6. _____ A person, such as a king, who is the head of a government.

7. _____ Having to do with England or Great Britain.

8. _____ To shoot a gun.

9. _____ The name of the group of people who make laws in England.

10. _____ To make or enact a law.

11. _____ A person who is chosen to help decide about laws for a group of people, a state, or a country.

12. _____ Control or government by a person, group, or country.

13. _____ Money that has to be paid to a government.

14. _____ To cancel or do away with a law.

15. _____ To give something, such as food or supplies, to a person or group of people.

16. _____ The killing of many people in a cruel way.

17. _____ Free from the control of another person or country.

18. _____ To let someone do something.

Choose five of these words. Write a sentence using each word. Be sure that each sentence starts with a capital letter and ends with a period. Write your sentences on a separate piece of paper.

The Colonists Begin to Protest

The Colonists and the British

Until the end of the French and Indian War, the people in the thirteen English colonies were happy with British rule. After the war, however, many colonists began to dislike their British rulers. There were several important reasons for this change in the way the colonists felt.

The Proclamation of 1763

One reason the colonists began to dislike British rule was the *Proclamation of 1763*. In this Proclamation, the king of England said that all the land west of the Appalachian Mountains belonged to the Indians. He said that colonists could not settle there. The colonists had fought the French to win these lands. Many colonists did not obey the Proclamation and settled in the new lands.

The Stamp Act

A second reason why the colonists disliked British rule was the *Stamp Act.* The French and Indian War cost a lot of money. Protecting the new lands was also expensive. The British needed to raise money. They thought the colonists should pay taxes to help pay for the war and for the protection the British army gave them.

The English Parliament passed several tax laws. One of these laws was the Stamp Act, passed in 1765. This law said that written material, such as newspapers and birth certificates, must be printed on special paper. The paper had a "stamp" or seal pressed into it. The colonists had to pay a tax when they bought the stamped paper.

British stamps used under the Stamp Act.

Colonists from nine of the colonies met together. They asked the king and Parliament to repeal, or stop, the Stamp Act. They said it was not fair to have *taxation without representation.* This means that, if colonists had to pay taxes to the British, then they should also be allowed to send representatives to vote in the British Parliament. The Stamp Act was finally repealed, but the king and Parliament did not agree about giving the colonies representation. The king and Parliament continued to make the colonists pay many other taxes. And they refused to let the colonists be represented in Parliament.

The Boston Massacre

Colonists and Soldiers: The Boston Massacre

A third reason why the colonists disliked British rule was that the British kept many soldiers in the colonies. The British forced the colonists to provide houses and food for the soldiers. Many colonists disliked the soldiers. Many soldiers disliked the colonists. In Boston, in 1770, some colonists threw snowballs at a group of soldiers. The soldiers fired their guns and killed five colonists. The colonists called this the *Boston Massacre.* The news of it made many people in all the colonies very angry with the British.

The Boston Tea Party

The Tax on Tea

A fourth reason why the colonists disliked British rule was another kind of tax. This was a tax on things that colonists had to buy from England. One of these things was tea. In those days people drank much more tea than coffee. The tea was imported, or brought in, from England, and the British collected a tax on every pound of tea that was sold in the colonies.

In 1773, a group of colonists in Boston decided to make a protest against the tea tax. They dressed up as Indians and got onto British ships in Boston harbor that had cargoes of tea. They threw all the tea into the water to show that they would not buy tea from England. This protest was called the *Boston Tea Party*.

The Intolerable Acts

A fifth reason why the colonists disliked their British rulers was a group of laws that the colonists called the *Intolerable Acts*. These laws were passed in 1774. They were meant to punish the people of Boston for the Boston Tea Party. They took away many of the people's rights. One of these laws closed the port of Boston. No ships were allowed to go in or out of Boston harbor until the tea was paid for. The Intolerable Acts made many people in the thirteen colonies believe that the British would never let them have more freedom.

Colonists Think About Independence

In conclusion, many American colonists became very unhappy with British rule. Some Americans began to think that the thirteen colonies should be an independent country. That way, they would be free of British rule forever.

Protesting the Intolerable Acts

UNDERSTANDING WHAT YOU READ: Comprehension Check

Read each statement. Write **T** for *True,* **F** for *False,* or **NG** if the information was *Not Given* in the story. Do not look back at the story until you have completed all 15 items.

1. _____ The colonists were happy with the Proclamation of 1763.

2. _____ The Proclamation of 1763 said that the colonists could settle in the Indian land west of the Applachians.

3. _____ The British thought that the people in the thirteen English colonies should help to pay for the French and Indian War.

4. _____ The Stamp Act said that people had to print newspapers and other materials on stamped paper.

5. _____ The British government canceled the Stamp Act.

6. _____ Some important people in England thought that the colonies should send representatives to vote in Parliament.

7. _____ The British kept many soldiers in the thirteen colonies and forced the colonists to provide houses and food for them.

8. _____ Angry colonists killed five British soldiers in the Boston Massacre.

9. _____ The colonists drank more tea than the English people did.

10. _____ The Boston Tea Party caused the tea tax.

11. _____ Indians threw tea off British ships into Boston harbor.

12. _____ The Intolerable Acts were meant to punish the people of one city in the colonies.

13. _____ Under the Intolerable Acts, ships could not use any harbor in the thirteen colonies.

14. _____ After the Intolerable Acts, some Americans thought that the colonies would never have more freedom.

15. _____ In 1774, all Americans believed that the colonies should be an independent country.

When you have completed all fifteen items, turn back to the story, "The Colonists Begin to Protest." Check each answer by scanning the story.

The War for Independence Begins

The First Continental Congress

The Intolerable Acts made most people in the thirteen colonies very angry. The colonists decided that they must act together. In the fall of 1774, twelve of the colonies sent delegates to Philadelphia to talk about their problems. This meeting was called the First Continental Congress. It was the first time that representatives of almost all the English colonies on the continent of North America had come together in one place.

Most of the delegates to the First Continental Congress were still loyal to the king of England. They believed that Parliament was to blame for the problems of the colonies. Some of the delegates were not loyal to the king. They believed that the colonies should become independent if the king and Parliament did not agree with the colonies' demands.

The First Continental Congress decided that the thirteen American colonies:

1. would *not* obey the Intolerable Acts;
2. *would* ask Parliament for more freedom to govern themselves;
3. would *not* buy anything from England or sell anything to England;
4. *would* fight the British if necessary.

The British Respond Angrily

These decisions of the First Continental Congress made the king of England very angry. Most of the members of Parliament were angry, too. They declared that the colony of Massachusetts was "in rebellion" against England.

The king and Parliament did not give the colonists more freedom. Instead, they decided to punish them. Parliament sent an order to General Gage, the governor of Massachusetts. The order said, "Stop the rebellion. Use force if necessary."

Lexington and Concord

The War for Independence started in Massachusetts in the spring of 1775. The colony's fighters were called *minutemen* because they could be ready to fight in one minute. The minutemen had war supplies in Concord, near Boston. General Gage sent soldiers from Boston to take these supplies away from the colonists. Paul Revere, a colonist from Boston, warned the colonists that the British were coming, so the minutemen were ready.

The British soldiers went first to Lexington, which was on the way to Concord. There was fighting in Lexington between the soldiers and the minutemen. Eight minutemen were killed and several others were wounded and could not go on fighting. There was more fighting at Concord, and the British never found most of the war supplies there. Finally, the British soldiers returned to Boston.

Nearly one hundred Americans were killed or wounded that day. About 250 British soldiers were also killed or wounded. It was the beginning of the American Revolution or the War for Independence.

MAP SKILLS

Look at the map on this page. About how many miles did the British soldiers march to get to Concord?

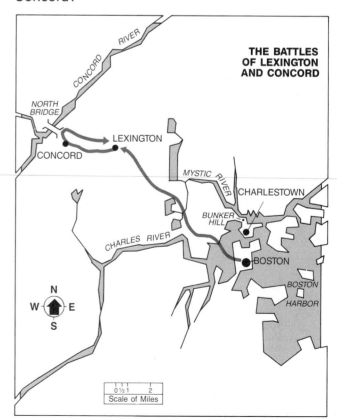

UNDERSTANDING WHAT YOU READ: Using Context

You can often understand what a new word means by using its "context." This means looking at the words and sentences that come before and after the word, and guessing what the word probably means.

Find the following words in "The War for Independence Begins" on page 82. Write a definition, or meaning, for each word. Work with a partner or a group to make your definitions as accurate as possible.

A minuteman

1. congress _____

2. continental _____

3. delegate _____

4. demands _____

5. loyal _____

6. rebellion _____

UNDERSTANDING WHAT YOU READ: Identifying Main Ideas and Details

The sentences below tell about "The War for Independence Begins." In each group, one sentence tells the main idea of that section. The other sentences tell interesting details. Write the letter **M** in front of the sentence that tells the *main idea*. Write **D** in front of the sentences that tell *details*.

1. The First Continental Congress

   _____ The First Continental Congress met in the fall of 1774 in Philadelphia.

   _____ People from twelve of the thirteen colonies went to the First Continental Congress.

   _____ The First Continental Congress said that Americans would fight if the British did not give them more freedom.

2. The British Respond Angrily

   _____ Parliament decided to punish the colonists and use force, if necessary, to stop the protests.

   _____ Parliament sent its orders to the British governor of Massachusetts, General Gage.

   _____ Parliament said that the colony of Massachusetts was "in rebellion" against England.

3. Lexington and Concord

   _____ A minuteman was a colonist who could be ready to fight in one minute.

   _____ Paul Revere told the colonists that British soldiers were on the way to Lexington and Concord to take war supplies away from the colonists.

   _____ The first two battles in the War for Independence were at Lexington and Concord.

   _____ About 100 Americans and 250 British soldiers were killed or wounded in the battles of Lexington and Concord.

Declaring Independence

BEFORE YOU READ: Using Section Headings

Look at the title of the reading and the section headings, and look up any unfamiliar words in the glossary. Then try to answer these questions.

1. What do you think happened at the Second Continental Congress?

2. What do you think the Declaraton of Independence said?

Discuss these questions with a friend and agree on your answers. Then read the paragraphs below to check your answers.

The Colonies Declare Independence

The Second Continental Congress

The battles of Lexington and Concord took place on April 19, 1775. Less than a month later, on May 10, 1775, another Continental Congress met in Philadelphia. This time there were delegates from all thirteen colonies. This Second Continental Congress established a Continental army with men from each colony in **it**. George Washington, who was one of the American leaders in the French and Indian War, was made Commander-in-Chief of the "Army of the United Colonies."

Although they established an army to fight the British, most of the delegates were still loyal to the king of England. **They** did not want to be independent. They wanted to continue to be colonists. But they wanted the British government to stop doing the things that made the colonists angry.

The king and Parliament would not listen to the colonists. **They** sent more soldiers to America. There were more battles. The colonists began to believe that England would never give **them** the freedom they wanted. They would have to become independent.

In June of 1776, the Second Continental Congress decided that the thirteen colonies should be independent from Britain. They asked a delegate named Thomas Jefferson to write a declaration, or statement, that would explain why they wanted to be independent from Britain.

The Declaration of Independence

The statement that Jefferson wrote is called the Declaration of Independence. The Second Continental Congress accepted **it** on July 4, 1776. The United States celebrates July 4 every year as Independence Day, the day that Americans declared that they wanted to be an independent nation.

The Declaration of Independence has three main parts. The first part describes the American colonists' ideas about government. It says that a government gets its powers from the consent, or agreement, of the people that it governs.

The second part of the Declaration of Independence explains why the colonists decided to separate from England. **It** lists the things that the king of England had done that the colonists believed were unfair.

The third part of the Declaration says that the colonists had asked the British many times to stop doing these unfair things. It says that the British continued to do **them**, however. Because of this, it says, "the representatives of the United States of America" declare their complete independence from England.

UNDERSTANDING WHAT YOU READ: Using Context

In the reading "The Colonies Declare Independence," seven words have been underlined and numbered. Each of these words stands for, or takes the place of, another word or group of words. On the lines below, write the underlined words and the word or group of words they stand for. The first one is done for you.

1. _it_   _the Continental army_ _____

2. ___ _____

3. ___ _____

4. ___ _____

5. ___ _____

6. ___ _____

7. ___ _____

UNDERSTANDING WHAT YOU READ: Identifying Main Ideas and Details

1. Tell two important things that the Second Continental Congress did.

_____

_____

2. Who wrote the Declaration of Independence? _____

3. Why is July 4 a holiday in the United States? _____

_____

4. What does each part of the Declaration of Independence say?

Part 1 _____

_____

_____

Part 2 _____

_____

Part 3 _____

_____

ACTIVITY: The Declaration of Independence

Listen to your teacher read the following excerpt, or selection, from the first part of the Declaration of Independence. New words are defined on the right. Now sit with a classmate and take turns reading these sentences to each other. Pronounce the words carefully and think of what they mean as you are reading. After practicing several times, memorize this excerpt at home. Recite it to a group of four or five classmates.

"We hold these truths to be self-evident: that all men are created equal, that they are endowed by their Creator with certain unalienable rights, that among these are life, liberty, and the pursuit of happiness. That, to secure these rights, governments are instituted among men, deriving their just powers from the consent of the governed."

self-evident: clear
created: made
endowed: given
Creator: God
unalienable: not to be given up
pursuit: search
secure: keep safe
instituted: established
deriving: getting
just: fair
powers: control
consent: agreement
governed: people

Signing the Declaration of Independence

The American Revolution

BEFORE YOU READ: Vocabulary

battle	defeat	navy	treaty
commander	fort	surrender	troops

Before you read "The War for Independence, 1775–1783," be sure you know these words. Check your knowledge by matching them with their definitions. Use the glossary at the end of this book or a dictionary if you need to.

1. _____ The leader of an army.

2. _____ A written agreement between two countries.

3. _____ A fight between two armies.

4. _____ To beat someone in a war or battle.

5. _____ To give up to an enemy and stop fighting.

6. _____ A place with strong walls to protect soldiers.

7. _____ Groups of soldiers.

8. _____ A group of ships belonging to a government and used for fighting.

ACTIVITY: Vocabulary Game

Read four definitions to your friend. Your friend has to say the word that matches each definition, without looking at the book! Give one point for each correct answer. Then your friend will read the other four definitions to you, and you will say the word that matches each definition.

My friend's score	

My score	

The War for Independence, 1775–1783

The War for Independence started in Lexington, Massachusetts, in 1775. It lasted for six years. Two more years passed before England signed a treaty with the United States. You have already read about the battles of Lexington and Concord. This chart shows some of the most important events that happened after those two battles.

EVENT	WHERE	WHEN	WHAT HAPPENED
Battle of Bunker Hill	Charlestown (Boston) MA	June 1775	British attacked Americans at fort. British won, but many British soldiers killed.
Crossing the Delaware; Battles of Trenton and Princeton	Trenton and Princeton, NJ	Dec. 1775 Jan. 1776	British took New York City. Washington's army went to Pennsylvania. Crossed Delaware River Christmas night and surprised British at Trenton; took more than 900 prisoners. Americans also won at Princeton on January 2.
Battle of Saratoga	Saratoga, NY	Oct. 1777	British General Burgoyne lost battle; surrendered more than 5000 troops to Americans.
Winter at Valley Forge	Valley Forge, PA	1777 1778	Washington's army spent cold, hungry winter in Valley Forge. Many Americans died of cold, illness, hunger. British army comfortable in Philadelphia.
France enters war		Feb. 1778	France sent supplies, soldiers, navy. Marquis de Lafayette helped Washington.
Battle of Charleston	Charleston, SC	May 1780	Americans badly beaten by British General Clinton and army of 14,000. Worst American defeat in war.
Battle of Yorktown	Yorktown, VA	Oct. 1781	Washington attacked Yorktown by land; French navy attacked by sea. British General Cornwallis surrendered. End of fighting in the war.
Treaty of Paris	Paris, France	Sept. 1783	Peace treaty between England and U.S. Gave independence to 13 colonies. U.S. owns all land east of Mississippi River and north of Florida. Spain owns Florida.

UNDERSTANDING WHAT YOU READ: Map Skills

Look at the map on page 77. Find the cities where the six battles took place. Write the date of each battle next to the city name. Also write the date for the battles of Lexington and Concord.

WRITING REPORTS

Look at the chart on page 88. Use the information to write a short report about the American War for Independence. Remember to write complete sentences. Begin a new paragraph for each event. The first sentence is done for you.

The War for Independence

The Battle of Bunker Hill was fought in Boston, Massachusetts in June, 1775.

_____

_____

_____

_____

_____

_____

_____

_____

_____

_____

_____

_____

_____

_____

_____

_____

_____

_____

_____

George Washington: An American Hero

Washington's Boyhood

George Washington was born in 1732 in the English colony of Virginia. His father owned a large plantation. The Washington family was wealthy, but they worked hard for their money.

Young George went to school for about eight years. He especially liked mathematics. He also learned about other parts of the world as he studied history and geography.

Washington Chooses an Occupation

George decided to become a surveyor, a person who measures land and makes maps of it. Surveyors use mathematics, which George liked. At that time, surveyors also traveled a lot. George thought that surveying would let him see other parts of the thirteen English colonies. He started work as a surveyor in 1747, when he was fifteen.

At first, George Washington helped older surveyors, but by the time he was 17, in 1749, he worked alone. He made quite a lot of money and began to buy land for himself.

Soldier and Farmer

In 1753, George Washington joined the Virginia militia, or army, and fought in the French and Indian War. He became a leader of the army in this war. After the war, Washington got married. He spent most of his time running Mount Vernon, a large farm that belonged to his family.

Commander of the Continental Army

When the thirteen colonies decided to fight the British in 1775, they chose George Washington to be the commander of the "Continental Army." The colonists trusted him because they knew that he was brave, truthful, and a good military leader.

Washington led the American army in many battles during the War for Independence. The British won many of the battles, but Washington kept his army fighting. In the winter of 1777–1778, Washington's army was camped at Valley Forge, in Pennsylvania. They were cold, hungry, and sick. Washington stayed with his men. He trained and encouraged them. He even used his own money to pay them.

Finally, in 1781, at Yorktown, Virginia, Washington's army, with the French army and navy, surrounded a large British army. Lord Cornwallis, commander of the British army, surrendered, and the British stopped fighting. The War for Independence was over.

Farmer and Citizen

After the war, George Washington went back to Mount Vernon. He was an excellent farmer, and he did many things to make his land better. In 1787, however, his country needed him again. He went to a meeting in Philadelphia to set up a better government. We call this meeting the Constitutional Convention, because the Constitution, the most important law in the U.S., was written there. Americans still live under that Constitution. Washington was made president of the Convention.

President of the United States

After the Constitution had been approved by the states, Washington was chosen to be President of the country. George Washington was the first person to be called President of the United States. Until 1789, the country was governed by a Congress, with a set of rules called the Articles of Confederation.

Washington was President from 1789 to 1797. He worked hard to make the new country strong. To help him, he chose a group of advisors, which people called his Cabinet. We still use the word Cabinet to describe the heads of the different government departments.

Retirement to Mount Vernon

After eight years as President, Washington was glad to go home to Mount Vernon. He died there two years later, in 1799. People all over the United States were sad that they had lost such a good leader. A year later, the capital city of the United States was established. George Washington had helped to plan it, and it was called Washington after him.

George Washington was very much loved and looked up to by Americans of his time. One of them summed up the way they felt: "First in war, first in peace, and first in the hearts of his countrymen."

UNDERSTANDING WHAT YOU READ: Making a Time Line

A time line shows important dates and events. You are going to make a time line of the life of George Washington. Fill in important events in Washington's life. First, write the date. Next to the date write a sentence that tells why that date is important. Washington's birth and death have been filled in for you. Write at least seven other events in the same way.

Date	Event
1725	
1730 *1732*	*Washington is born in Virginia.*
1735	
1740	
1745	
1750	
1755	
1760	
1765	
1770	
1775	
1780	
1785	
1790	
1795	
1800 *1799*	*Washington dies at Mount Vernon.*

Developing Reports: Heroes of the War for Independence

Many brave men and women helped the United States become independent. You will learn about some of these heroes by reading, writing, presenting, and listening to reports about them.

John Paul Jones

Ethan Allen

Sybil Ludington

Patrick Henry

Paul Revere

1. Read this report about one of these heroes, Sybil Ludington. Notice that the report is organized into an *introduction*, a *body*, and a *conclusion*.

Sybil Ludington

Introduction
Tells what the report is about.

This report is about Sybil Ludington. She was a hero in the American War for Independence because she rode alone on horseback for more than 40 miles to tell people to come and fight the British.

Body
Gives the important points and some details about the hero's life.

The first important thing about Sybil Ludington is that she was very brave. Sybil was only 16 years old in 1777, but she rode all night for more than 40 miles to tell people that the British had come to Danbury, a town in Connecticut not far from her home. She knew that she could be caught by the British, but she went just the same.

The second important thing about Sybil Ludington is that her ride stopped the British. British soldiers had captured Danbury and set its houses on fire. They planned to march west to the Hudson River and capture the land on both sides of it. But Sybil kept this from happening. She rode ahead, in the direction the British army planned to go. She stopped at every house and called out, "Danbury's burning! The British are coming! Meet at the Ludingtons!" More than a thousand men came. Sybil's father led a large army of colonists. The colonists fought and turned back the British soldiers just outside Danbury.

Conclusion
Tells what the report was about and why the hero was important.

In conclusion, this report has been about the American hero, Sybil Ludington. Sybil was important in American history because, as a 16-year-old girl, she bravely rode all night for more than 40 miles to warn people that British soldiers were nearby. The people answered Sybil's warning. They came together to fight the British and the British were forced to turn back.

2. Now your teacher will help you choose one of the other heroes to write a short report about. You will need to do some research on the hero you choose. Ask your teacher or your librarian where to find information. As you read about your hero, take notes on the important facts.

Write your report on the next page. Some sentences have been started for you. Use your best handwriting, because later you will read your report to a group of classmates. Remember to indent the beginning of a paragraph, to start sentences with a capital letter, and to end sentences with a period, a question mark, or an exclamation point.

TITLE OF REPORT _____

Introduction

This report is about _____ .

He (or she) was a hero in the American War for Independence because _____

_____ .

Body of Report

(Write the most important things that happened in the life of this hero. Write dates and places of birth and death, if known. State one or two reasons why the person was important; for each main reason, give one or two details that tell what the person did.)

_____

_____

_____

_____

_____

_____

_____

_____

_____

_____

_____

Conclusion

In conclusion, this report has been about the hero _____ ,

who was important in American history because _____

_____

3. Now you are going to present your report to a group of classmates. Read over what you have written, and correct it carefully. Then practice reading it aloud at least five times. You can practice reading it to a friend or someone in your family, or you can make a tape recording and play it back. Check these things about your oral reading:

    a. Do I read too fast, too slow, or about right?

    b. Do I read too loud, too soft, or about right?

    c. Do I pronounce words and phrases so that others can understand me?

    d. Is my report well organized so that others can follow my ideas?

When you are satisfied that you can do your best on your oral report, read it to a group of classmates who have not studied the same hero. They will take notes on what you say.

4. Now it is your turn to listen to the oral reports of three of your classmates. They will report on the three heroes that you did not study. Listen carefully to each report, and take notes on the important points. Use the space below to take your notes.

Report 1

Name of Hero _____

What this hero did to help the War for Independence _____

_____

_____

Other important facts _____

_____

_____

Importance of this hero _____

_____

_____

_____

_____

_____

Report 2

Name of hero _____

What this hero did to help the War for Independence and other important facts

_____

_____

_____

_____

_____

Importance of this hero _____

_____

_____

_____

Report 3

Name of hero _____

What this hero did to help the War for Independence and other important facts

_____

_____

_____

_____

_____

Importance of this hero _____

_____

_____

_____

American Cities Grow

Boston, 1775

ACTIVITY: Line Graphs

A line graph is a useful way of showing how something changes during a period of time. Look at the box. It shows information about the population of three cities from 1730 to 1790. Then look at the three line graphs. They show the same information in a different way.

Independence Hall
Philadelphia, 1770

	New York	Philadelphia	Boston
1730	8,500	8,500	13,000
1750	13,300	13,400	15,731
1770	21,000	28,000	15,520
1790	33,131	42,444	18,038

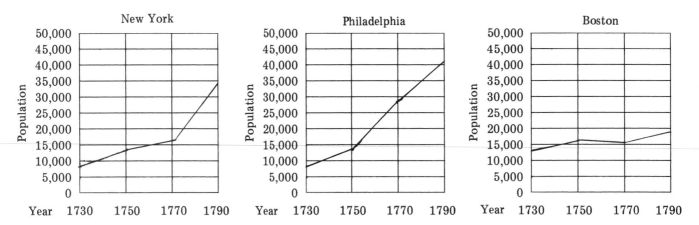

To make a line graph, you put numbers for the things you are going to graph up the side. On the graphs on this page, the numbers show population. You put periods of time across the bottom. On the vertical (up and down) line for each year, a dot shows the population for that year. A straight line joins the dots. The population figures are not in even 5,000s, so the exact location of the dot on the line is an estimate, or careful guess. For example, the population of New York in 1730 was 8,500. You know that this is between 5,000 and 10,000, and that it is nearer to 10,000 than it is to 5,000. So the dot is a little more than halfway up in the space between 5,000 and 10,000.

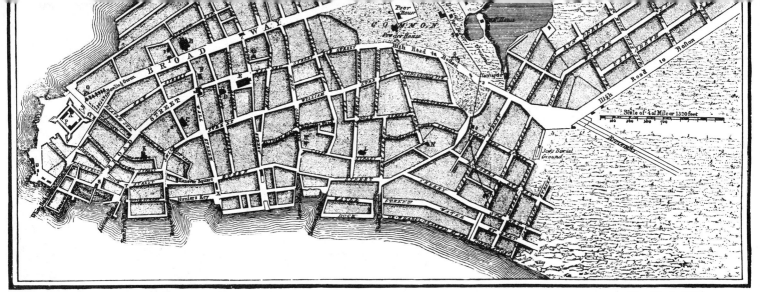

New York, 1767

Look at the graphs on page 96. Answer these questions.

Which of these cities was the biggest in 1730? _____

Which was the biggest in 1750? _____

Which grew the fastest from 1730 to 1790? _____

Which two cities were nearly the same size in 1730 and 1750? _____

Now make a line graph for the population of Charleston, South Carolina. Use the information in the box and make your graph on the "grid."

Charleston	
1730	4,000
1750	8,000
1770	10,863
1790	16,359

Charleston, 1776

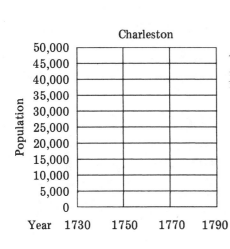

Charleston

Population: 50,000 / 45,000 / 40,000 / 35,000 / 30,000 / 25,000 / 20,000 / 15,000 / 10,000 / 5,000 / 0

Year: 1730 1750 1770 1790

The United States Constitution

BEFORE YOU READ: Vocabulary

Before you read "The Constitution," be sure you know these words.

amend	To improve; to make something better by changing it.
amendment	An improvement; something added to a document to change it and make it better.

The Constitution

Two Important Documents

The United States Constitution and the Declaration of Independence are the two most important documents in the history of the United States. You have already learned about the Declaration of Independence. It said that the United States was a free country and would not be ruled by England any more. Now you are going to learn about the Constitution.

The Constitution is a plan of government. When the thirteen colonies first became independent states, each state had its own government. These thirteen governments worked together under a plan called the Articles of Confederation.

The Constitutional Convention

After several years, people in the thirteen states decided that the Articles of Confederation needed some changes. Twelve of the states sent delegates to a meeting in Philadelphia in 1787 to amend, or improve, the Articles of Confederation. Instead, the delegates wrote a whole new plan of government. This new plan was the Constitution. We call this meeting the Constitutional Convention.

The Three Parts of the Constitution

There are three important parts of the Constitution. The first part tells how the government is organized into three branches or sections. You will read more about the three branches on page 100. The second part is the Bill of Rights. This is ten amendments, or improvements, that were written in 1789, two years after the first part of the Constitution. They describe rights that all citizens of the United States have. The third part of the Constitution is the other amendments that have been added since the Bill of Rights was written.

The amendments are numbered. Numbers 1 to 10 are the Bill of Rights. The other amendments are numbers 11 through 26. Number 11 was approved in 1798. Number 26 was approved in 1971.

The Bill of Rights

The Bill of Rights is especially important because it tells people, in writing, that they have some very special rights. It says that they can follow the religion that they choose. It says they can speak freely. It says they can meet together to discuss their ideas. It says that newspapers and magazines cannot be stopped from printing things that the government doesn't like. The Bill of Rights gives rules to protect people who are accused of crimes. These rules make sure that the people have a fair trial. Finally, the Bill of Rights says that the people and the states have many other rights. It says that the government cannot take these rights away.

The Other Amendments

The last part of the Constitution is Amendments 11 through 26. These amendments were written to keep the Constitution up to date as the United States grew and changed. A very important amendment is number 13, which was approved in 1865. This amendment says that there will be no slavery in the United States. Amendment 15 (1870) gives all male (men) citizens in the United States the right to vote. This amendment was added to make sure that men who had been slaves could vote. Amendment 19, approved in 1920, gives women the right to vote. The most recent amendment, number 26, approved in 1971, allows any citizen who is 18 years old or older to vote. This means that younger people can have influence in the government.

The Importance of the Constitution

The Constitution is a very important document because it has provided a plan of government for the United States for more than 200 years. Only 26 changes, or amendments, have been made in the Constitution since it was written. These changes helped to keep the Constitution up-to-date. The United States Constitution is also important because it has been the model for the constitutions of other new nations.

UNDERSTANDING WHAT YOU READ: Comprehension Check

Complete the following sentences about the United States Constitution.

1. The document that tells how the United States is governed is the _____.

2. The Constitution was written _____ years after the Declaration of Independence.

3. The part of the Constitution that tells about the three branches of government was

    written in the year _____.

4. Another name for Amendments 1 through 10 is the _____.

5. The rest of the Amendments were written over a period of _____ years.

6. Amendments 1 through 10 say that Americans have the right to follow the _____

    that they choose, to _____ freely, to _____ together to discuss ideas, and

    to have a _____ trial. It says that newspapers and magazines cannot be stopped

    from _____,

    and it says that the people and the states have _____.

7. The Amendment that gave freedom to slaves in the U.S. was passed in the year

    _____.

8. Women were given the right to vote _____ years after the Bill of Rights was written.

9. The last Amendment is especially important for _____.

10. Two reasons why the U.S. Constitution is important are:

    a. _____

    b. _____

The Three Branches of Government

The national government that was set up by the Constitutional Convention has three branches or parts. Each branch has certain powers, or things that it can do. Each branch can also check, or stop, the actions of the other branches in certain ways. The boxes on this page show the powers of the branches.

The Capitol

LEGISLATIVE BRANCH—CONGRESS

The legislative branch has the power to
- make laws,
- declare war,
- approve or disapprove of people that the President appoints or gives jobs to,
- remove a Supreme Court judge,
- remove the President.

EXECUTIVE BRANCH—THE PRESIDENT

The executive branch has the power to
- manage, or run, the government,
- carry out the laws and make people obey them,
- suggest new laws,
- command the army and navy,
- appoint Cabinet members, Supreme Court judges, and other officials,
- approve or disapprove of laws made by Congress.

The White House

The Supreme Court Building

JUDICIAL BRANCH—THE SUPREME COURT

The judicial branch has the power to
- decide what a law means,
- decide if a law agrees with the Constitution or disagrees with it,
- decide if actions of the President agree with the Constitution or disagree with it,
- settle arguments between the states,
- protect the rights of the people.

In addition, Supreme Court judges serve for life and cannot be removed by the President.

UNDERSTANDING WHAT YOU READ: Comprehension Check

Answer these questions about the powers of the three branches of government.

1. Which branch can veto or stop a law made by Congress? _____

2. Which branch can say that Congress has made a law that is against the Constitution?

   _____

3. Which branch can stop the appointment of a Supreme Court Judge? _____

4. Which branch can fire or get rid of the President? _____

5. Which branch can get rid of a Supreme Court judge? _____

6. Which branch can say that something the President does is against the Constitution?

   _____

7. Which branches of government have to think about laws? _____

8. Which branch can choose people for important jobs? _____

9. Which branch decides if the United States Government will go to war against another

   country? _____

10. When two states cannot agree, which branch decides which is right and which is wrong?

   _____

ACTIVITY: Finding Out About Your Government

The President and the members of Congress are elected, or chosen by the
voters, for certain lengths of time, or terms. Then there is another election.
Do some research and complete these sentences.

1. The Congress has two parts or "houses," the Senate and the House of Representatives.

   Senators (members of the Senate) serve for a term of _____ years.

2. Representatives (members of the House of Representatives) serve for a term of

   _____ years.

3. The President serves for a term of _____ years.

4. The next election for a President will be in _____.

5. The name of the President now is _____.

6. The names of the two senators from your state are _____ and

   _____.

7. The name of the representative for your part of your state is _____.

Benjamin Franklin

LISTENING AND TAKING NOTES

You are going to hear about Benjamin Franklin, one of the most important people in the early history of the United States. As you listen to the information about Franklin, write notes on the T-list below. Write only the key words that will help you remember the facts. You do not have to write complete sentences.

MAIN IDEAS	DETAILS

A. Life as a boy and young man

An early printing press

1. Born _____, in _____.
   (year)
2. Went to school for _____ years.
3. When 10, _____.
   Taught self _____, _____, many languages.
4. When 12, _____.
5. When 17, _____.
6. When 24, _____.

B. Things Franklin was famous for

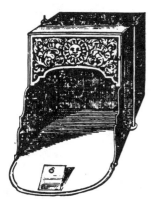

The Franklin stove

1. _____
   a. Published newspaper in _____.
   b. *Poor Richard's Almanac*, ideas about _____.
   c. _____ about his first fifty years.
2. _____ and _____
   a. Experiments in _____.
   b. Invented _____.
   c. Invented _____.
3. _____
   a. Founded Philadelphia library and _____.
   b. 1757 to _____. Stayed _____.
      Helped people to _____.
   c. 1775, delegate to _____.
      Helped plan _____.
   d. 1783, _____.
   e. 1789, delegate to _____
      _____. Helped write _____.

A lightning rod

C. Important to early history of U.S.

1. _____.
2. _____.
3. _____.

In his brother's print shop

The kite experiment

The Philadelphia library

Signing the United States Constitution

A New Nation **103**

A. Circle the letter of the correct answer.

1. The colonists said, "No taxation without representation" because of the:
   a. Stamp Act   **b.** Boston Massacre   **c.** Boston Tea Party   **d.** Intolerable Acts

2. Colonists threw tea into the Boston harbor because they:
   a. were celebrating American independence   **b.** liked coffee more than tea
   c. thought the tea tax was wrong   **d.** were protesting the Proclamation of 1763

3. The British punished the colonists for the Boston Tea Party by:
   a. holding the Boston Massacre   **b.** putting a tax on tea
   c. giving the colonists representation in the British Parliament
   d. passing the Intolerable Acts

4. The First Continental Congress said that the American colonies would:
   a. be independent and free of Great Britain
   b. each send a representative to the British Parliament
   c. not fight the British   **d.** not obey the Intolerable Acts

5. The fight for independence began in:
   a. Boston in 1772   **c.** Philadelphia in 1774
   b. Valley Forge in 1777   **d.** Lexington in 1775

6. The Second Continental Congress did two important things. One was to declare the thirteen colonies independent from Great Britain. The other was to:
   a. establish an American army   **b.** dress as Indians and throw tea in Boston harbor
   c. write the Constitution to govern the nation
   d. elect George Washington as President of the United States

7. The document that tells about peoples' "unalienable rights" to "life, liberty, and the pursuit of happiness" is the:
   a. Constitution   **b.** Bill of Rights
   c. Treaty of Paris   **d.** Declaration of Independence

8. The Bill of Rights is an important part of the:
   a. Stamp Act   **b.** Judicial Branch
   c. Constitution   **d.** Declaration of Independence

9. The President can control the powers of Congress by:
   a. appointing Cabinet members and Supreme Court judges
   b. suggesting laws for Congress to pass   **c.** disapproving laws made by Congress
   d. running the government

10. The power to decide what a law means and whether it follows the Constitution belongs to:
    a. all three branches of government   **b.** the Legislative branch
    c. the Executive branch   **d.** the Judicial branch

B. Write your answers.

1. The Declaration of Independence says that governments get "their just powers from the consent of the governed." The British government did many things in the thirteen colonies without "the consent of the governed." Name three of these things.

   a. _____

   b. _____

   c. _____

2. In what part of the Declaration of Independence did Thomas Jefferson list these things, the first part, the second part, or the third part?_____

C. Look at the map on page 70 and the graphs on page 96, and use them to answer this question. The first Continental Congress, the Second Continental Congress, and the Constitutional Convention were all held in Philadelphia. Why do you think the colonists chose Philadelphia for these meetings? Give two reasons.

   a. _____

   b. _____

D. What Do You Think? Discuss these questions with a friend, a small group, or the class.

   • Some of George Washington's soldiers wanted him to be king of the United States. He refused. Later, he was elected President. What do you think is the difference between a king and a President? Why do you think Washington refused to become the king?

   • In 1777, the flag of the United States had thirteen stars. Today the flag has 50 stars. What do the stars stand for? How many stripes are there? What do they stand for?

   • The United States government has three branches, legislative, executive, and judicial. Which do you think is the most powerful branch of government? Why do you think so?

E. Role Play

Imagine that you are living in the colonies in the 1770s. Write conversations that might have taken place between the following people. Work with a small group of friends. Write enough parts so that everyone in your group has something to say. After your group has written and practiced the conversations, you can perform one of these short plays for the class.

1. You live in Boston. You have just heard about the tax on tea. Some of you are very angry about it. Some of you think the tax is a nuisance, but you like tea and are willing to pay the tax. Discuss why you think the tax is fair or unfair, and what you will do.

2. You live in Lexington. It's after midnight. Paul Revere has just warned you that British soldiers are marching from Boston. Another family has come to your house to talk with your family about what you will do tomorrow morning. Write the conversation.

3. You live in Philadelphia. The Second Continental Congress is going to meet there next week. Some of you think that they are wrong. Discuss what you would like the Second Continental Congress to do and what you think it will do.

Glossary

The words in this glossary have been defined according to the way they are used in this book. You may want to check your dictionary for other meanings. The pronunciation key is from Thorndike-Barnhart Intermediate Dictionary by E.L. Thorndike and Clarence L. Barnhart. Copyright ©1974 Scott, Foresman and Company. Reprinted by permission.

a	hat, cap	f	fat, if
ā	age, face	g	go, bag
ä	father, far	h	he, how
b	bad, rob	i	it, pin
ch	child, much	ī	ice, live
d	did, red		
		j	jam, enjoy
e	let, best	k	kind, seek
ē	equal, be	l	land, coal
ėr	term, learn	m	me, am

n	no, in
ng	long, bring
o	hot, rock
ō	open, go
ò	order, all
oi	oil, voice
ou	house, out
p	paper, cup
r	run, try

s	say, yes
sh	she, rush
t	tell, it
th	thin, both
TH	then, smooth
u	cup, butter
ù	full, put
ü	rule, move
v	very, save

w	will, woman
y	young, yet
z	zero, breeze
zh	measure, seizure
ə	represents:
	a in about
	e in taken
	i in pencil
	o in lemon
	u in circus

advisor (ad·vī′zər)-Someone who gives advice and helps you make decisions.

agree (ə·grē′)-To have the same opinion or idea.

agreement (ə·grē′mənt)-A written or spoken understanding; a statement of how things will be done.

allow (ə·lou′)-To let someone do something, to let something happen.

amend (ə·mend′)-To improve or correct a document.

amendment (ə·mend′mənt)-A section that is added to a document to change and improve it.

appoint (ə·point′)-To place someone in a special job.

approve (ə·prüv′)-To say something is good, to agree with.

army (är′mē)-A large group of soldiers organized and trained to fight.

attack (ə·tak′)-To suddenly begin a fight.

average (av′rij)-Ordinary; in the middle.

battle (bat′(ə)l)-A fight between two groups of soldiers.

bay (bā)-Part of a sea or lake partly surrounded by land.

border (bôr′dər)-The edge of a state, country, etc.; the line between two states, countries, etc.

British (brit′ish)-Having to do with England.

cargo (kär′gō)-A load of goods that are carried by ship, truck, train or airplane.

capital (kap′ə·təl)-1. City that is the center of government for a state, country, etc. 2. Upper-case: *capital* letters - A, B, etc.

capture (kap′chər)-To take and hold as a prisoner.

celebrate (sel′ə·brāt)-To have a party or feast in honor of someone or something.

chief (chēf)-The leader: the chief of a tribe, the chief of police, etc.

claim (klām)-1. To say something belongs to you, your country, etc.: to *claim* the land for Spain. 2. Something a person or country says it owns.

climate (klī′mit)-The kind of weather that a place generally has.

coast (kōst)-The land next to the ocean or sea.

colonist (kol′ə·nist)-Someone who lives in a colony.

colony (kol′ə·nē)-A place settled by a group of people and under the rule of the mother country.

commander (kə·man′dər)-The leader of an army.

companion (kəm·pan′yən)-A person who travels or stays with another person; a friend.

congress (kong′gris)-A meeting of delegates to make laws or political decisions.

conquer (kong′kər)-To defeat or win control of through war. - con′quer·or

constitution (kon′sti·t(y)ü′shən)-A document that sets up a government and describes the parts of the government and their responsibilities.

continent (kon′tə·nənt)-One of the seven large land areas of the earth: Europe, Asia, Africa, Australia, North America, South America, Antarctica.

control (kən·trōl′)-To rule or have power over.

convention (kən·ven′shən)-A political meeting.

convince (kən·vins′)-To make someone believe something or agree with you.

council (koun′səl)-A group of people who discuss, give advice about, or make laws.

crops (krops)-Plants grown for food or money.

culture (kul′chər)-The entire way of life of a particular people, their customs, language, tools, etc.

declaration (dek′lə·rā′shən)-An announcement.

declare (di·klär′)-To announce.

defeat (di·fēt′)-To beat someone in a battle or war.

delegate (del′ə·gāt)-A representative chosen by people to go to a meeting and vote for them.

demands (di·mandz′)-Requests that must be met, rights that must be given.

democracy (di·mok′rə·sē)-A form of government in which the people rule, either by voting directly or by electing representatives.

desert (dez′ert)-A dry region often covered with sand.

discover (dis·kuv′ər)-To find or find out about a place or a thing before anyone else.

document (dok′yə·mənt)-A legal, written statement.

domestic (də·mes′tik)-Tame, raised by people: *domestic* animals.

emperor (em'pər·ər)-The ruler of an empire.

empire (em'pīr)-A group of territories ruled by one government.

equal (ē'kwəl)-Having the same rights.

equator (i·kwā'tər)-An imaginary line that goes around the middle of the earth.

establish (ə·stab'lish)-To set up or found.

estimate (es'tə·mit)-A careful guess about numbers.

evergreen (ev'ər·grēn')-Having leaves that stay green all year long.

expedition (ek'spe·dish'ən)-A journey made to find or explore something.

exploration (eks'plə·rā'shən)-The exploring of a new area in order to learn about it.

explore (ik·splôr')-To travel through a place in order to learn more about it.

farm (färm)-1. To grow crops or raise animals for food.
2. Land used for growing crops and raising cows, sheep, etc.

farmer (fär'mər)-A person who owns or works on a farm.

feast (fēst)-A big meal with special food.

fire a gun-To shoot a gun.

forest (fôr'ist)-A large area covered with trees.

fort (fôrt)-A place with strong walls built to protect soldiers.

found (found)-To set up or establish: *found* a colony.

freedom (frē'dəm)-The right to think, act, speak, etc. as you wish.

fur (fer)-The soft, hairy coat of an animal.

government (guv'ər(n)·mənt)-The group of people or the system that controls or rules a state, country, etc.

governor (guv'ər·nor)-The person who governs a territory, colony, etc.

gulf (gulf)-A large bay.

harbor (här'bər)-A port.

harvest (här'vest)-1. To gather and bring in a crop. 2. The crops gathered in one season.

hemisphere (hem'ə·sfir)-One half of the earth's surface: the northern and the southern *hemispheres*.

herd (herd)-A large group of one kind of animal: a *herd* of cows.

hero (hē'rō)-A person who does something brave to save other people or help his/her country.

hibernate (hī'bər·nāt)-To spend the winter sleeping, as bears and other animals do.

hunter (hun'tər)-A person who kills wild animals for food or sport.

igloo (ig'lü)-A dome-shaped hut built by Eskimos, usually of blocks of hard snow.

import (im·pôrt')-To bring goods or products into a country.

in the distance-Far away.

independent (in'di·pen'dənt)-Free from the control of another person or country.

inland (in'lənd)-Not near the coast.

intolerable (in·tol'ər·ə·bəl)-Too much to endure, more than you can stand.

inventor (in·ven'tər)-Someone who builds something entirely new and different.

island (ī'lənd)-A body of land entirely surrounded by water.

latitude (lat'ə·t(y)üd)-The distance north or south of the equator. Latitude lines run east-west on the globe.

law (lô)-A rule established by a government that all the people must obey.

legend (lej'ənd)-A story that has come down from earlier times and is thought by many people to be true.

locate (lō'kāt)-To find where something is.

loyal (loi'əl)-Believing in and standing up for a person, country, or idea.

lumber (lum'ber)-Trees that have been cut into boards for use in building.

majority (mə·jôr'ə tē)-More than half of a given group of people.

make a living-To work and earn money.

massacre (mas'ə·kər)-The killing of many people in a cruel way.

migrate (mī'grāt)-To move from one country or region to another to settle.

migration (mī·grā'shən)-The movement of people from one country or region to another to settle.

mine (mīn)-A large hole or deep tunnel made for removing minerals from the earth.

mineral (min'ər·əl)-Substance such as coal or gold found in the earth that people put to use.

mission (mish'ən)-A working and living place set up by missionaries, people sent to convert other people to a certain religion.

mountain (moun'tən)-A high land, higher than a hill, with peaks and steep sides.

mouth of a river-The place where a river flows into the ocean.

native (nā'tiv)-Born, grown, or first living in a particular area: *Native* Americans, *native* crops.

natural resources-Raw materials provided by nature: forests, minerals, water supplies, etc.

navigation (nav'ə·gā'shən)-The art of steering a ship from one place to another.

navy (nā'vē)-A group of ships belonging to the government and used for fighting.

New World-North and South America.

obey (ō·bā')-To do as you are told.

occupation (ok'yə·pā'shən)-A job or career.

ocean (ō'shən)-Great bodies of salt water that cover 70% of the earth's surface.

oral (ôr'əl)-Spoken, out loud.

palace (pal'is)-A large building where kings, queens, etc. live.

Parliament (pär'lə·mənt)-The name of a group of people who make laws in England.

pass a law-To make or enact a law.

permanent (per'mən·ənt)-Lasting forever, or for a very long time.

plantation (plan·tā'shən)-A large farm where just one crop is grown (cotton, rice, etc.)

population (pop·yə·lā'shən)-The number of people living in a place.

port (pôrt)-A city or place where ships come and go; harbor.

powerful (pou'ər·fəl)-Having great strength.

priest (prēst)-A church leader; a person who leads the religious services in certain churches.

prisoner (priz'(ə)n·ər)-Person captured by the enemy.

proclamation (prok'lə·mā'shən)-An official announcement, as of a new law or course of action.

product (prod'əkt)-Something grown or made and sold.

protest (prō'test)-Words or actions that show a person is against something.

provide (prə·vīd')-To give a person or group of people some things they need.

rebellion (ri·bel'yən)-An uprising or fight against the government or person in control.

region (rē'jən)-An area of land with certain features and climate.

repeal (ri·pēl')-To cancel or do away with a law.

report (ri·pôrt')-1. A written account giving information about something.   2. To give information either by telling or writing it.

representative (rep'ri·zen'tə·tiv)-A person who is chosen by a group of people to help make decisions about laws.

revolution (rev'ə·lü'shən)-A war that is fought to overthrow the ruling government.

rights (rīts)-Things that the law allows people to have, things people believe they should be able to do or have.

ruins (rü'inz)-The remains of buildings that have been destroyed through time, war, etc.

rule (rül)-1. To control or govern.   2. Control or government by a person, group, or country.

ruler (rü'lər)-A person, such as a king, who is the head of a government.

sail (sāl)-To travel in a boat or ship that is pushed by the wind.

sailor (sā'lər)-A person who works on a boat or ship.

scientist (sī'ən·tist)-A person who studies things in nature and does experiments to understand how and why they work.

search (sėrch)-To look very hard; to try to find something.

seasons (sē'zənz)-The four parts of the year: spring, summer, fall, winter.

select (si·lekt')-To pick or choose.

settle (set'əl)-To establish a home or colony.

slave (slāv)-A person owned by another like a piece of property.

soldier (sol'jer)-A person who is part of an army and trained to fight.

spring (spring)-The season after winter and before summer.

supplies (sə·plīz')-Things that are needed, such as food, clothes, and weapons.

surrender (sə·ren'dər)-To give up; to admit you have lost a battle or war.

tax (taks)-Money that has to be paid to a government.

temperature (tem'pər·ə·chər)-The amount of hotness or coldness in something, number that tells how hot or cold it is.

territory (ter'ə·tôr·ē)-An area of land owned by a person or country.

tobacco (tə·bak'ō)-A plant whose leaves are dried and used for smoking in pipes, cigarettes, etc.

trade (trād)-The buying and selling of goods.

transport (trans·pôrt')-To move something from one place to another.

trap (trap)-To catch an animal with a hidden device, usually made of metal.

treaty (trē'tē)-A written agreement between two countries.

tribe (trīb)-A group of families living together, sharing a culture and having one chief or leader.

tundra (tun'drə)-Land in the far north that stays frozen most of the year.

valuable (val'y(ü·)ə·bəl)-Worth a lot of money.

voyage (voi'ij)-A journey, usually on a ship or boat.

wood (wùd)-The hard part of a tree, under the bark.

wounded (wünd'əd)-Hurt in battle.

Learning Strategies

The lesson plans for the Student Book activities present and practice the following learning strategies. For further discussion of these strategies, please refer to the Teacher's Guide.

Student Book pages

Metacognitive Strategies

Advance Organization — 8–9, 11, 16–19, 21–23, 29, 31, 34–37, 44–47, 50–53, 55–56, 66–71, 76–77, 79–85, 90–91, 98–99
Previewing the main ideas and concepts of the material to be learned, often by skimming the text for the organizing principle.

Advance Preparation — 26–27, 40–43, 48–49, 61–63, 65, 86, 92–95, 104–105
Rehearsing the language needed for an oral or written task.

Organizational Planning — 40–43, 61–63, 65, 88–89, 92–95
Planning the parts, sequence, and main ideas to be expressed orally or in writing.

Selective Attention — 12–15, 18–22, 24–25, 30–47, 52–57, 60–67, 70–73, 78–85, 88–103
Attending to, or scanning key words, phrases, linguistic markers, sentences, or types of information.

Self-Evaluation — 10, 14–15, 23, 26–27, 32–33, 36–43, 48–49, 52–54, 57–59, 61–64, 68–75, 78–89, 92–105
Judging how well one has accomplished a learning activity after it has been completed.

Cognitive Strategies

Contextualization — 10, 14, 30, 32–33, 36–37, 44–45, 54, 60, 78, 82–83, 87, 98–99
Placing a word or phrase in a meaningful sentence or category.

Elaboration — 12–13, 26–27, 31, 36–39, 44–45, 48–49, 51–53, 55–56, 60–63, 66–67, 70–75, 79–81, 90–91, 98–101, 104–105
Relating new information to what is already known.

Grouping — 10, 16–19, 25, 30, 60, 88–89, 96–97
Classifying words, terminology, or concepts according to their attributes.

Imagery — 12–13, 18, 21–22, 29–35, 38–47, 51–53, 58–60, 66–67, 70–73, 77, 82–83, 88–91, 96–97, 100–105
Using visual images (either mental or actual) to understand and remember new information.

Student Book pages

Inferencing — 11–15, 18–19, 21–23, 26–27, 31, 34–37, 40–49, 51–57, 66–75, 77–87, 90–99, 104–105
Using information in the text to guess meanings of new items, predict outcomes, or complete missing parts.

Note-taking — 20, 24, 32–33, 40–45, 57–59, 61–65, 90–95, 100–103
Writing down key words and concepts in abbreviated form during a listening or reading activity.

Resourcing — 10, 18–19, 32–37, 40–43, 46–47, 58–59, 64–67, 70–71, 78, 84–85, 87, 92–95, 100–101
Using reference materials such as dictionaries, encyclopedias, or textbooks.

Summarizing — 20, 24, 32–33, 57–59, 64, 79–81, 84–85, 88–89, 102–103
Making a mental or written summary of information gained through listening or reading.

Transfer — 8–9, 12–13, 16–17, 23, 25, 31, 34–39, 44–45, 50, 52–53, 55–56, 76–81, 87, 90–91, 98–99, 104–105
Using what is already known to facilitate a learning task.

Social Affective Strategies

Cooperation — 10, 14, 16–20, 23–27, 29–33, 36–49, 52–54, 57, 60, 64–67, 70–73, 76–87, 90–105
Working together with peers to solve a problem, pool information, check a learning task, or get feedback on oral or written performance.

Questioning for Clarification — 31, 40–43, 54, 57, 61–63, 79–81, 86, 88–89, 92–97, 100–101
Eliciting from a teacher or peer additional explanation, rephrasing, or examples.

Academic Skills

This index lists academic skills emphasized in the Student Book activities. Additional practice in these skills is often provided in preparatory and follow-up activities in the Teacher's Guide lesson plans.

Student Book pages

Listening and Speaking Skills

Discussing issues, supporting opinions — 22, 23, 27, 37, 39, 49, 57, 58–59, 67, 75, 84, 105
Preparing and giving oral presentations — 27, 43, 49, 62, 75, 86, 94, 105
Understanding oral presentations — 20, 24, 33, 43, 62–64, 94–95, 102

Reading Comprehension Skills

Comparing and contrasting — 19, 35, 47, 57, 66, 67, 71, 72, 73, 96, 101, 105
Determining meaning through context — 14, 32, 46, 83, 85
Drawing conclusions, predicting outcomes — 15, 23, 35, 37, 42, 47, 53, 67, 84, 92–93, 99, 101, 105
Drawing inferences, making generalizations — 11, 23, 27, 35, 47, 49, 58–59, 67, 71, 75, 99, 105
Incorporating information from illustrations, maps, graphs — 14, 15, 19, 21, 25, 32, 34–35, 38–39, 41–43, 45, 47, 58–59, 66–67, 71, 72–73, 82, 88–89, 96–97, 100–101, 102–103, 105
Recalling details — 15, 23, 26, 27, 37, 48, 49, 53, 57, 69, 74, 75, 81, 83, 85, 92–93, 99, 101, 104, 105
Recognizing or inferring main idea — 11, 15, 22, 23, 26, 37, 41–42, 48, 49, 53, 58–59, 69, 74, 75, 81, 83, 85, 92, 93, 99, 104, 105
Recognizing cause and effect — 19, 23, 27, 35, 47, 49, 67, 105
Recognizing same information phrased differently — 15, 22, 26, 37, 53, 99, 101
Relating one's own experiences to the material — 17, 23, 25, 27, 34, 37, 39, 49, 58–59, 60, 61–62, 66, 75, 101, 105
Scanning for specific information — 14, 15, 19, 37, 45, 46, 53, 57, 69, 71, 81, 83, 85, 91, 99, 101
Skimming for an overview of material — 11, 44, 52, 84
Synthesizing and elaborating, making judgments — 23, 25, 27, 34, 37, 41–42, 47, 49, 60, 67, 75, 105

Map Skills

Charting locations and routes on a map — 27, 31, 37, 38, 39, 43, 45, 49, 53, 57, 69, 71, 75
Comparing two maps — 18, 34, 39, 43, 45, 71, 72, 73
Identifying continents and oceans — 18, 21, 27, 31, 34, 38, 49, 66, 72
Identifying the equator, the hemispheres — 34, 49, 66, 72
Locating places on a map — 17, 18, 21, 29, 37, 38, 41–43, 45, 47, 53, 57, 66, 69, 71, 72, 73, 88, 105
Understanding cardinal (compass) directions — 18, 21, 38, 66, 69
Understanding latitude lines — 34, 49, 66
Using map keys, scale of miles — 14, 17, 18, 21, 29, 31, 34, 37, 39, 43, 45, 51, 57, 69, 71, 72, 73, 77, 82

Study Skills

Alphabetizing — 25, 30
Classifying — 19, 25, 30, 52, 60
Interpreting and constructing bar graphs, line graphs, data charts, time lines — 19, 35, 41, 45, 47, 57, 65, 67, 88, 91, 96, 101
Organizing notes into a report — 41–42, 65, 88–89, 92–93
Taking notes from oral presentations — 20, 24, 43, 62–63, 64, 102
              reading selections — 45, 57, 92
Using a dictionary or glossary — 10, 32, 36, 46, 54, 78, 84, 87
Using an encyclopedia or reference book — 37, 39, 65, 75, 92, 101

Writing Skills

Organizing and writing a report — 40–42, 65, 88–89, 92–93
Summarizing — 20, 24, 32–33, 42, 47, 57, 58–59, 64, 65, 85, 92, 96–97, 102
Transforming graphic information into sentences — 21, 42, 47, 67
Writing complete sentences — 11, 23, 42, 65, 67, 71, 78, 88–89, 91, 93
Writing definitions — 14, 83
Writing instructions — 61–62
Writing paragraphs — 42, 65, 88–89, 93